THE PONY BOOK

Books by the Author

THE BOOK OF HORSES AND HORSEMANSHIP

THE HUNTING DOGS OF AMERICA

THE PONY BOOK

JEFF GRIFFEN

THE PONY BOOK

•

ILLUSTRATIONS BY
JEANNE MELLIN HERRICK

1966

DOUBLEDAY & COMPANY, INC.

GARDEN CITY, NEW YORK

CONTENTS

THE PONY BOOK

Kids love ponies! Four-year-old Chuck Turner of Baytown, Texas, proudly shows off his Shetland pal.

Chapter 1

The Pony Today

Of all the domesticated animals we have, few can steal the heart much quicker than a pony. There's spritely magic about the way he frolics in a pasture or carries a youngster in an exploration of secret places or elegantly draws an adult in a diminutive carriage at a gala show.

We here in America have more varieties of ponies and do more with them than any other country on earth. In recent years they have come to provide as much true fun, if not more, than the horse, for everything about them is easier to do and it's done on a more pixyish scale. Furthermore, ponies bring out the best in people, as parents who have involved their children with them know. There is no juvenile delinquency around ponies, rather the reverse of it, creativity, interest, concern, responsibility, and the like.

These are a few of the reasons why since World War II the pony world has expanded beyond the expectations, even the dreams, of its most enthusiastic followers. In the two decades from 1945 to date, registered ponies have more than quadrupled, grade ponies almost doubled. The consequences have been the appearance of new trainers, new equipment, new classes at horse shows, the rise of all-pony shows, of "using" ponies, of racing ponies, midget ponies, and much more.

Age-old breeds like the Shetland have been bred away from their chubby coarseness into a spectacular refinement that makes them the little jewels of the horse world. New breeds such as the Pony of the Americas and the Americana have been created to meet the widening interests of pony followers. Other breeds like the Connemara from Ireland and the Galiceño from Mexico (followers prefer to call this latter a small horse though it falls within pony height qualifications) have been successfully introduced into the United States. All have added luster and prestige to the ever-widening world of ponies and give every indication of continuing to do so.

Like our whole country, the pony world has changed its makeup considerably in recent years. Before World War II large stables of show ponies—Hackneys and the like—were maintained by the very wealthy who made

Adults love ponies too! Here are the Royal Roadsterettes, a ladies' drill team of the Island Empire Shetland Pony Club, Spokane, Washington. Members perform at state fairs and children's benefits, range in age from twenty to eighty. The flag bearer here is Mrs. Ruby Wainright, a great-grandmother. Others left to right are Mrs. Olive Catlin, Mrs. Carol Davidson, Mrs. Bertha Slinkard, Mrs. Phyllis Drake, Mrs. Donna Hulett, Mrs. Helen Holman, Mrs. Evelyn Thompson, Mrs. Dorothy Blackmer, Mrs. Dorothy Horseman, and Mrs. Vera Defreeze. Drill Master is Mr. Rex Blackmer.

major importations and showed as a pleasurable pastime what appeared to be a dying bauble of the horse world. A trainer, an assistant trainer and several grooms were employed to maintain the elaborate establishment.

Then in the 1950s, as individuals across the country acquired more leisure time and affluence, the pony began to draw a wider following. People from all walks of life wanted an animal they could compete with, one that required skill and dexterity in handling, that was small and easily-kept, yet elegant. The answer was the pony which, as a result of training, became a bundle of supreme beauty and under harness in the show ring required all the trappings of bygone splendor.

As interest in ponies widened, new uses and applications were found for them. Those ponies which had good action but were a shade too coarse or long of neck to win fine harness classes made good-looking roadsters. Thus roadster pony classes sprang into being, patterned after those of the Saddle Horse in light harness. In judging these events, the cry "Turn 'em on!" became the signal to trot the ponies at full speed so the judge could observe how they maintained their gait and form. Since the driver was dressed in racing silks and rode a miniature racing sulky, it wasn't long before the ponies hit the tracks and began racing like their big cousins, the Standardbreds. Thus the pony world has grown to duplicate just about every facet of the horse world.

Many large stables still exist today. In fact, there are more than ever before. Some are incorporated as businesses, some are operated for advertising, some for pleasure. Across the country are scattered herds of 25 to 200 ponies, and when properly managed and promoted, they yield a good return as an investment. But a member of the vast new group of pony followers owns from one to five head, although any pony fancier admits that once the bug has bitten, the tendency is insatiably toward buying more.

This modern indoor arena for training ponies is at Danby Farm, outside of Omaha, Nebraska. Mrs. Daniel Langfeld, Jr., drives Shetland Ch. Patton's Look Alike. In background, professionals Del Graham and Jack Deakins practice stretching a harness pony.

Especially nowadays, for the show rules require that entries remain longer on the grounds. The Shetland exhibitor begins to watch the Welsh or Hackney classes in his long hours of waiting and the first thing he knows he's bought a second breed to compete with. And why not, since he'll go to the show anyway! Hauling one more pony won't make any difference.

Many professional people, doctors, lawyers, and the like, show Hackneys or Shetlands as a relaxing and exciting hobby. Many farmers have found they can make a better living raising good Welshes than good corn, but they quickly discover that the real money in ponies is in show stock and they too follow the shows across the country. Many enterprising families with a few acres of land have made ponies an avocation, much to the joy of their children who were sent to college on the proceeds.

As a result of individual interest in ponies, many trainers have successfully established stables where they take ponies at a monthly rate of about $75 and fit them out for showing. This term means training and preparing them for the major horse shows, pony shows, and fairs around the country. Usually the owner himself will handle a young pony in "in-hand" or model classes the first two years of its life. Then, lacking the time and facilities, he gives the pony to a trainer who introduces it to the ways of driving, whereupon it becomes either a harness of a roadster pony depending upon its looks and ability. After the pony has been trained a year or two, the owner takes it back and reaps the full enjoyment of showing and competing with it himself, usually in amateur classes.

Many pony farms train their own ponies to the point where the amateur can buy and begin showing immediately. Also, some auctions feature performance ponies of the highest quality—roadsters, fine harness, racers—and from here a buyer can obtain a finished animal ready for competition. Trainers often have them for sale but they seldom compete with ponies which they themselves own. At a large show such as Devon or the Chicago International the prize money will amount to $1000 or more in a single open stake class, so the professional not only has a good incentive for winning but also must have his animal razor-sharp in order to win.

From the above it is obvious why the pony has developed a great following among adults, almost as great as among children. When prices for a well-trained, registered pony range from $500 to $2500 and on up into five figures for an outstanding champion herd sire, obviously children cannot afford such an investment or take the proper care of it.

Years ago a child's pony was nearly always of the "grade" type—unregistered and of unknown breeding. He may have looked like a Shetland or a Welsh, even been passed off as such. Probably forty percent of our pony stock today falls into this category. They are used for pleasure riding, general youthful fun, for pony rides at twenty-five cents each during the summer at carnivals and playgrounds. Their ranks are fast declining, however, for a registered pony can be had for just a little higher price, and it is certainly worth the difference in value, pride of ownership, and especially the right to show them.

For this last reason more and more parents have involved their children in registered show ponies of all descriptions, from fine harness and roadsters to hunter types, parade and Western "using" ponies. From caring for their ponies and entering competitive events, children develop great pride in their mounts, treat them with respect. They experience the thrill of winning, the disappointment of losing, acquire the courage to try again. Such experience, gained early in life, helps the child to grow in constructive directions, channels his energies into healthy patterns which deeply affect his life whether or not he ever sees a pony when he grows up.

Proof of this, and another exciting facet of pony use, lies in the fields of mentally retarded and delinquent children. Ponies do something good to kids, allow them to come out of themselves, communicate, and learn. Shetlands and Welshes are being used more and more in specialized school programs. By touching, leading, and eventually riding a pony, a mentally retarded child "feels" deeply for this animal and loves it. When the child

Up and over! Nine-year-old Susie Dent and her Ch. Connemara Pony, Whitewood Muffin, take a timber fence together.

comes across a picture of the pony in a book, he is able to assimilate the information much more readily whether it be adding or learning to dress himself. As a consequence new levels of communication and instruction are being reached in this field. Ponies are also being used in programs to teach delinquent children responsibility, respect, pride. Here again association with a lovable Shetland brings out qualities of personal worth that psychology, discipline, and adult communication too often cannot reach.

Since this book is the first of its kind to be entirely devoted to all breeds of ponies and all phases of their modern-day activities it must cover a lot of territory. It must describe the pony world for the outsider who may find it exciting enough to become a devotee; it must provide information for the pony buff already engaged in showing, racing, and/or raising ponies; it must also deal with two levels of interest—the adult and the young adult. Therefore, if at times the material seems overly clear or obvious, the reader is asked to be patient and understand that someone with less background or knowledge may find the same passage of value. With this in mind let's move into a definition of the word *pony,* which is not really definable in the eyes of many authorities today.

The rule has long been and still generally prevails that any equine under fourteen-two hands (fifty-eight inches) is a pony, but many breeders claim their animals are small horses rather than ponies. They provide elaborate distinctions between the two on the basis of conformation and/or personality, and in many cases their claims are justified. For the sake of clarity, however, the long-standing definition will be applied throughout this book

A proud winner in Indian costume is Donna Bridge of Stillwater, Oklahoma, riding Chief Little Britches, a Pony of the Americas, which is one of our newest breeds. Note that the pony wears no bridle or bit, only a leather thong in the mouth as the Indians used.

and every breed under fourteen-two hands will be discussed whether it be a small horse, a pony, or a burro.

The average pony height ranges between forty and fifty inches. Miniature ponies are thirty-two inches or under. All breeds of horses have within themselves various strains which tend to produce small offspring. This accounts for the Thoroughbred ponies, the Tennessee Walking ponies and the Saddlebred or Gaited ponies. In a sense they are not true ponies because they may, as likely as not, produce horse-sized offspring when bred, but they too will be discussed in this book.

In order to understand and appreciate the pony one must know his history. It is, of course, the history of the horse and a most fascinating one because we can trace it so clearly through various stages of development through many eons of time. *Equus*, as he is scientifically called, did not first appear in the form he is seen today. He evolved through many

Pony chariot racing has become a popular sport at most all Pacific Northwest fairs. Here three teams of pony chariots come down the stretch full tilt and looking like real Romans.

trials and experiments of Nature into various sizes and stages, some successful, some falling by the wayside.

His first stage of which we have substantial record was in the Eocene Age and is called *Eohippus* or Dawn Horse. He stood no more than twelve inches at the shoulder, could run like the wind, and had four toes on his front feet and three on his back, each with a tiny hoof. Skeletal remains of *Eohippus* have been found in most parts of the world—eastern and western Europe, Asia, Africa, and the Western Hemisphere.

Babette Jenny of Unionville, Pennsylvania, proudly leads her brother Peter in Lead Line Class at the Devon Horse Show. Babette, now fourteen, is one of the East's best junior riders through her early training and association with ponies.

Eohippus was a browser, that is he lived in the forest, nibbling a diet of tender leaves and shoots of trees, his teeth being such that he could not masticate grasses. For some unknown reason, as *Eohippus* began to evolve in Europe, Asia, and Africa, he suddenly became extinct. The only surviving branch of the family remained in North America. Here he went through several stages of evolution, becoming first *Mesohippus,* then *Merychippus,* then *Pliohippus,* finally *Equus.*

Mesohippus, the Midway Horse, took on size and carried his weight mainly on his center toe which as a result became a sturdy hoof, the others dwarfing into sharp-toed nobs. *Merychippus* was the key stage of the horse's evolution. At this point he gained a tooth construction which allowed him to move from the forest to the plain and chew its tough grasses. This permitted him to survive the great land upheavals and probably accounts for our having a horse today. The European branch of *Eohippus* developed in a different direction, never achieved this dental refinement, and thus became extinct.

Pliohippus took on further size and his extra toes retracted into the long narrow splint bones which lie just under the skin on the horse's front and hind legs today. *Equus,* the last step in the process, took on more height and weight. Since his entire development took place in North America, this is generally accepted as his home.

The above evolutionary process, described in four paragraphs, actually crept along over an estimated sixty million years. At the beginning of the Ice Age, *Equus* was forced to roam, across the newly risen Isthmus of Panama into South America with the llama, across the Bering Peninsula into Asia with the then-diminutive camel. In time he spread into the farthest reaches of Europe and Africa, developed into several different species of wild asses, zebras, onagers, and various-sized horses.

Across the length and breadth of the world the horse flourished, except in his homeland here in America. By some quirk of fate or unknown epidemic, all the horses in North and South America were destroyed during our Ice Age, and since the Bering Strait had been formed, none could return from Asia. So the Western Hemisphere became barren of the horses it had nurtured, until the Spanish conquistadors brought them back in the early sixteenth century.

In western Europe the horse thrived as a wild animal. The magnificent cave drawings of Cro-Magnon man twenty thousand years ago in southern France show *Equus* as an alert and beautiful wild pony. At that time man hunted the horse for food, and the great Cro-Magnon trash heaps, one of which contains the bones of over a hundred thousand horses, prove the fact that he was of pony size at that time.

Gradually three distinct types emerged. The Middle-East, rather short,

Ponies can be kept in your backyard. Here a Shetland mare and colt cavort on the Rock 'n' Roll farm of Dr. and Mrs. Malcolm Teller, Maple Valley, Washington.

desert horse eventually became the highly refined Arabian-Barb. The tall, heavy-boned horse of the Central European plains became the huge war charger of armored knights during the Middle Ages, and draft animals in Europe and America later. The Celtic pony, small, sturdy, and unbelievably tough, spread throughout northern Europe, giving us the Norwegian Dun, Icelandic pony, and all the magnificent ponies of the British Isles.

Most of our American ponies come from the British Isles through this early Celtic type, but not all of them.

The horses that Cortés, de Soto, and other Spanish explorers brought to America, the famous Spanish jennets, were mostly of Arab and Barb blood

Hackney pony, King's Gaiety, owned by Colonel and Mrs. Frank Ryan of Ottawa, Canada, steps off with another championship win. The ribbon is traditionally held in the mouth of winning driver, which in this case is the well-known professional, Alf Jones. Right: The Alpenrose Dairy Cavalry, composed of kids and Shetlands, travels all over the West Coast for parades and exhibitions.

and around fourteen hands in height, thus really ponies. The Spaniards set up great horse and cattle breeding ranches on the islands of Jamaica, Cuba, and Hispaniola. From their expeditions into the mainland horses escaped, ran wild through the Carolinas and Virginia, where Indians captured them and gained mounts for the first time in their history. The settlers used them for farm work and for their quarter-mile racing. In time, they became the colonial Quarter-of-a-Mile race horses, foundation stock of today's Quarter Horse which is himself on the short side, averaging fifteen hands in height, only two inches above pony standards.

Horses escaped from Spanish haciendas in Mexico, Texas, and California and within a hundred years formed the gigantic herds of wild mustangs which roamed the prairies. Actually these animals were nearly always of pony size.

The vast majority of our ponies come from the British Isles, where for centuries they served in war and peace, not so much as playthings for children, but as sturdy workers pulling carts and plows, laboring underground in mines. The great value of ponies has always been their minimal upkeep and utility in a small area. They can forage for themselves and actually enjoy doing so. For the small farmer in England, Scotland, Ireland, the Shetland Islands, a large draft animal would not earn the value of his feed.

Ponies have been in America a long time. Many horses of pony size were brought over by the colonists, especially in the early days when a family had no idea of what lay ahead. A tough, sturdy pony of 13 or 14 hands was the most practical animal they could bring to the new world. It required less feed and was capable of almost as much work as a horse.

In time, the American vastness proved more suitable to a larger horse, particularly as settlements expanded and the country opened up, yet many people still clung to the pony, seeking different uses for it in a society dependent upon the horse for its transportation and power.

That magnificent bay horse from Vermont, Justin Morgan, born in 1789, gained fame for his beauty and ability to outtrot, outpull, outrun, out-work every other horse in his area. His offspring became the elegant carriage horses of the wealthy, the super trotters of the 1830s, 40s, and 50s, and produced our present-day Morgan horse breed which has spread across the country. His blood runs heavily in today's Standardbred trotter and pacer, circulates in many a Saddle Horse and Tennessee Walker, even Quarter Horse. All this from an amazing little animal only 14 hands high—in truth, a pony!

Often we fail to realize that the famous English Thoroughbred in its early stages was around 14 hands, or pony size. Only through judicious outcrossing and selective breeding was its height increased to the rugged 16 and 17 hands we know today.

As America grew, ponies appeared continually at livestock fairs and exhibitions in the 1870s. Importations from England and the Shetland Isles continued. In 1888 The American Shetland Pony Club was formed, five years before the august American Jockey Club. Included in the first volume of this pony stud book, published in 1893, were some Shetlands owned by "Buffalo Bill" Cody of North Platte, Nebraska.

Some men in the 1890s had the idea of selling flashy ponies to city people for pulling elegant little buckboards around town for shopping and other errands. All went well until bicycles came along.

In the course of time ponies became a luxury. With the rise of the automobile and during depressions, their ranks grew thin, though there was always a group who loved to breed and train and show them under harness for their miniature beauty. Historically the Midwest—Illinois, Iowa, Missouri, Indiana, Ohio—has been the heartland of the harness show pony, though his avid followers are now spread across the country.

The East, with its fox-hunting proclivities, has leaned more to children's ponies for pleasure riding, jumping, hunting, and equitation classes that follow the pattern of their parents at horse shows. These ponies, under English saddle, are miniature hunters in conformation and action.

But in the last two decades all facets of the pony world have grown so that one can hardly restrict any breed or type of pony to a region. California and Texas love the Hackney. The Pacific Northwest has taken the Welsh and Shetland to heart as well as chariot racing and chuck wagon racing. The South has become a second home for all types of show ponies, particularly the roadster. Kentucky and Tennessee boast of their Five-Gaited

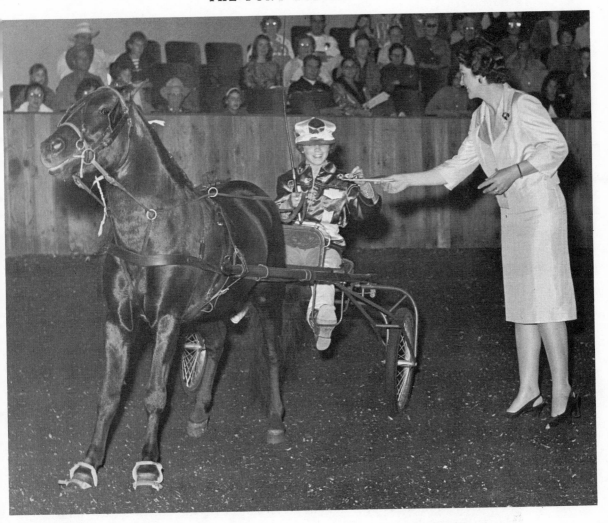

Pony Roadster Class is won by Gail Pratt, eleven, of Mercer Island, Washington, at Parade of Champions Show in Seattle. Says her father: "My kids have each had their own pony to handle, train, and take care of since they were four, and I might add that it would be hard to find a delinquent child among those with a pony to occupy their time."

and Walking ponies. New England, always the hotbed of trotters and pacers, has initiated and developed pony trotting with a passion.

To learn about ponies one must learn some of the terms associated with the horse world. If you ever buy a registered pony, the description on the pedigree is nearly always used to identify it. On some occasions a pony is tattooed, thus establishing permanent identification, but generally identification is done by describing the color, height, sex, and markings. Thus these terms must be clearly understood, for they pop up constantly at pony shows and auctions, in advertisements and on pedigrees.

Ponies come in a variety of colors—black, brown, bay, chestnut, sorrel, palomino, gray, white, dun, buckskin, pinto, and appaloosa.

To be called black, a pony must be one hundred percent so, except for white head or leg markings. Any fine brown hairs around the nostrils or flanks makes him brown. Sometimes only an expert can distinguish between the two.

A bay pony always has a black mane, tail, and legs, and his body color is generally reddish-brown. When his body color is yellowish-tan, he is called a light bay; when deep brown, a dark bay; when bright mahogany, a blood bay.

A chestnut pony has the same range of colors as a bay, except that his mane, tail, and legs are always the same color as his body, never black.

A sorrel pony is brilliant yellow, gold, or red and is distinguished from the palomino by having a mane and tail the same color as his body rather than the palomino's light or white mane and tail.

Gray ponies come in a wide variety of hues. Some are born black and shed into dark steel grays; others are born sorrel and shed into light grays. All gray ponies, as they grow older, become lighter in color, often ending up white or nearly so.

The true white pony is an albino with no pigment in hair, skin, or iris of the eye. They are rare and are not desired by most people.

A dun pony varies in color from yellowish-tan to mouse and almost always has black mane, tail, and legs and a black stripe down its back.

A buckskin is a light yellow pony, usually the result of mating "sand" and "blood" bays.

Pinto ponies that have white and black body markings are called piebald; those with white and any other color markings over the body are skewbald. Also named *calico, spotted,* and *paint,* they are generally referred to by specific colors in the pony show ring, i.e., "that bay-and-white gelding" or "the black-and-white mare."

Appaloosa-colored ponies come in six variations, the most common of which is dark body with a white blanket, covered with polka dots, across the rump. The other colors will be discussed in Chapter 5.

Some breeds have certain characterizing colors. Shetlands are famous for their silver, golden, and chestnut dapples, always accompanied by light or white manes and tails. Dapples are light-colored spots which appear against a dark background and provide a beautiful mottled effect. Thus, when you read on a pedigree "Color: Silver Dapple, WMT" you can be sure the pony is a startling gray covered with light dapples and possessing a white mane and tail as indicated by the *WMT* abbreviation.

"Black Points" is a term usually applied to bays or duns. It means they have black manes and tails, black legs, and often a dark stripe down the back, although this usually disappears as the pony grows to adulthood.

Head markings are the white spots and patches which appear on the face of the pony and are always listed on a pedigree. There are six basic markings, as shown in the adjoining head illustrations: star, snip, stripe, race, blaze, and bald. Combinations of these are often seen, the most frequent of which are Star-and-Snip, and Star-and-Stripe.

Leg markings are always white too. They consist of heel, coronet, half pastern, pastern, ankle, half stocking and full stocking patches as shown in the accompanying drawings. Thus if a pony has a full stocking on his near hind leg, you can be sure his left hind leg is white almost to the hock. On ponies that are ridden, particularly hunting ponies, the left side is always referred to as the near side, the right side as the off side. The near side is most easily remembered as the one you mount on. Harness ponies, since they are not ridden, are most often referred to in left and right terms.

The height of a pony is determined by measuring from ground level to top of withers. Generally, horses are measured in hands and ponies in inches, although you will often hear someone say his pony is thirteen-one or the like. This means thirteen hands and one inch. A hand equals four

Know your pony's head markings for proper identification. Shown left to right are: star and snip; stripe; star and stripe; blaze; bald.

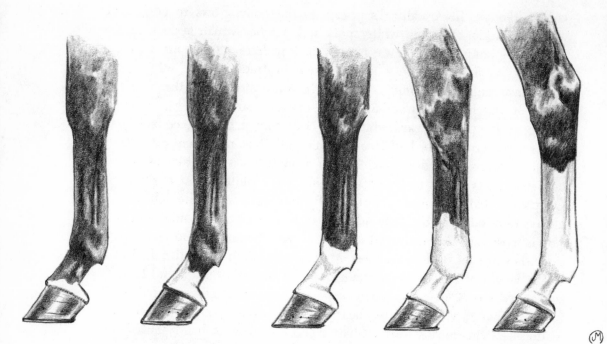

Know your pony's leg markings. Shown left to right are: front coronet; front pastern; front sock; rear half-stocking; rear full stocking.

inches, so to know the height in inches you multiply the thirteen by four and add the one inch, a total of fifty-three inches.

Pony gaits consist basically of walk, trot, and canter. A gallop is merely a fast canter. A Tennessee Walking pony has a running walk instead of a trot. A parade pony's parade gait is a high-stepping trot. Fine harness ponies like the Hackney have a park trot, a showy step that is the height of action and animation. These will be discussed further under the various breed chapters.

Action is a term you will hear wherever you go in the show pony world. This pony has superb action, that one has poor action. It refers to the manner in which the pony moves his legs, front and back. For each breed it differs, and for each pony it differs. Also, action can be changed to a considerable degree by shoeing. The heavier the shoe and the longer the hoof, the higher and more springy the action because the pony has to lift harder to get his foot off the ground.

A typy pony is one whose conformation closely reflects the ideal of the breed and is on the flashy, refined side. He may have bad manners or be a scatterbrain, but he'll always catch your eye. The opposite of this is a coarse pony which has a harsh or overdeveloped structure, and a weedy pony which is narrow-chested and sharp-withered.

A rangy pony has a long lean look and usually a slight build to go with it, but he's strong. The better trotting ponies tend to be like this, also roadster ponies, while the model and fine harness ponies had better not be.

Now for a short description of some of the show pony types. The breed chapters will cover them more completely, but a little background information is needed here.

A model pony is one that is shown on a lead and bitting rig by a handler and is meant to be a true representation of what the breed should be. He is judged on character and conformation, not performance. In an "in-hand" class he is judged usually sixty percent on conformation, type,

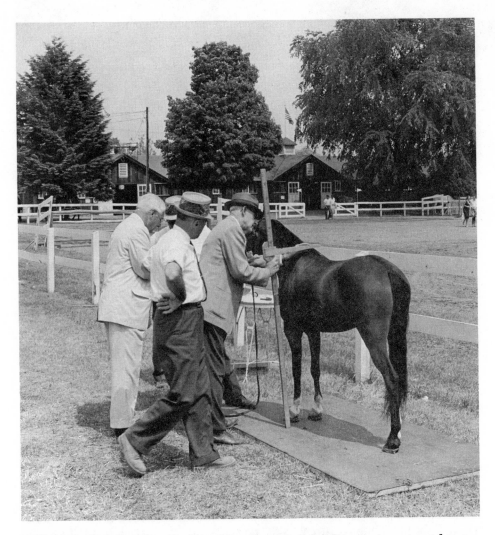

Official measurement of a pony. Height is determined by distance from ground to top of withers as shown here. Any equine 14 hands 2 inches (58 inches) or under is generally referred to as a pony.

Imported New Forest ponies come to the hand of Mrs. Betty Galloway for some corn. On left is English Ch. Jack Straw. Herd is owned by Mr. and Mrs. William Olmstead of Gloucester, Virginia.

quality, and finish, forty percent on way of going, disposition, and manners.

A harness pony is one that is shown under fine harness (lightweight) and pulls a viceroy in which the driver sits. Judging is done on manners, quality, and performance. If a champion model pony can also become a champion in harness, then he's a gem of rarity and considerable value.

A roadster pony is harnessed to a sulky, and his driver wears colorful racing silks in the ring. He is judged not so much on high action but on racing action, that is, manners, way of going, and how much speed he has while still maintaining true form.

A hunter-type pony is one that has the conformation of a hunter horse. He is used for following the hounds in fox hunting, hence is a good jumper, and is a popular contestant in the pony hunter classes at all the big Eastern shows. More about the breeding of these ponies later.

Some of the most beautifully matched pony teams through the years have been used by major companies for advertising. Shown here is the superbly matched, all-black six-pony hitch of the Victor Comptometer Corporation pulling a pony-size fire wagon.

One of the most important terms connected with pony talk is "sound." If a pony is declared sound by an owner or veterinarian, it means he is free of any blemish or injury or flaw that keeps him from operating at his full peak. Such physical faults as a splint, bowed tendon, ring bone, partial blindness, etc., would render the pony lame or incapable of complete exertion, and the buyer must be aware of such. These and other defects which make for "unsoundness" will be discussed in the chapter on "Buying a Pony."

The pedigree of a pony reveals its age, but if you buy one that doesn't have papers you will have to estimate how old it is or else have some knowledgeable person tell you. The easiest way to determine this is by studying the teeth.

A pony's teeth are a fascinating contrivance of Nature. His front incisors are used for cutting off or cropping grass, while his rear grinders do the masticating. Grass is a very tough substance which would wear a human's teeth out in just a few years. A pony's teeth wear off at a slow rate, but they continue to rise from the gums all the while so that a perfect bite is maintained throughout a lifetime of twenty-five to thirty-five years. Occasionally the teeth drift out of alignment, in which case a veterinarian files back the proper bite. This is called "floating" and often brings a skinny pony back to robust health.

A pony's baby teeth are called "milk" teeth. They begin to appear a week after birth and are shed over a period of five years for permanent ones. Until they are all replaced he is said to have a green mouth.

His permanent teeth have cups in them, and as long as all these cups are visible and not worn away he is said to have a full mouth. This is generally from five through nine years of age.

Once the cups are worn away from eating and grinding, usually after nine years of age, the pony is said to have a smooth mouth. At this time a mark called Galvayne's Groove begins to appear on the sides of his teeth and age can quite accurately be determined by it after that.

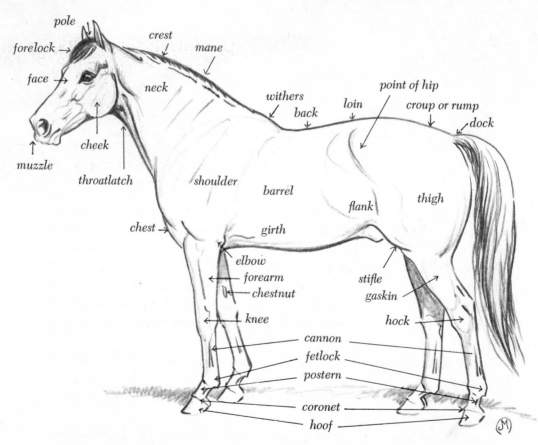

Know the correct name for the various parts of your pony.

Several other physical factors contribute to determining a pony's age. These will be discussed in the "Buying a Pony" chapter which also includes sketches of teeth according to age.

At this point it is important to learn the various parts of the pony so that when you hear them mentioned or read about them you know just what is being referred to. The diagram opposite lists the major parts and areas of the pony. They are the same for all breeds. In fact, the language is international.

Head study of first National Champion Shetland, Patton L, shown to his title by the late Harvey Heyl, and now senior sire at Danby Farms, Omaha, Nebraska.

Chapter 2

The Shetland

Short and rugged, with an iron constitution, dream of every child, star of the show pony world, of circus acts, of pony pulling contests and racing—such is the Shetland, most famous and widely used pony on earth today.

This lovable little animal is the smallest of all pony breeds as well as the most numerous. He's earned his popularity by being a friendly worker whether lugging a load of peat to town or flashing high-stepping form in front of a viceroy. Practicality has long been his middle name. From centuries of struggling to survive on the rugged Shetland Islands north of Scotland he has developed the nack, even the relish, of fending for himself. In winter he grows a thick bushy coat that provides ample protection against fierce storms and cold weather. He enjoys pawing through snow to forage. A shed suffices for his shelter. No shoeing is required for ordinary work or play.

This highly developed instinct for self-preservation, when coupled to his diminutive size, makes him ideal for children, particularly small ones. Often the tiny tots who ride him and play with him don't know the proper manipulations of equitation, yet he patiently perseveres. Even if a child falls off, it's likely to be no more than a slide of little height, so close is the average Shetland built to the ground. For this reason kids do more things with him and enjoy him far greater than they ever could a horse.

As his name indicates, this sturdy pony comes from the Shetland Islands, a lonely archipelago fifty miles north of Scotland and only 350 miles from the Arctic Circle. Because the islands are so barren and treeless and constantly raked by North Atlantic storms, only the toughest of people, sheep, cattle, and horses have survived. The native horse is the Shetland pony, a blocky, heavy-boned, draft-type animal.

The word *Shetland* or *Zetland* is a modernization of the old Norse *Hjaltland* which, authorities say, meant "highland." Of the hundred islands which compose the archipelago, only a quarter are inhabited. The largest, Mainland, which has one-half the total area, has a coastline so irregular that no point on the island is more than three miles from the sea.

Vikings, early inhabitants of the islands, are credited with bringing in the first ponies over two thousand years ago. By royal marriage the islands became the property of the Scottish crown in 1472, and thus are part of the British Isles today, although many Norse traditions, names, and folklore remain part of the culture.

The Shetland pony was probably a small fellow when the Vikings brought him to his new home and because of rugged environment he certainly didn't take on any size. He shrank, if anything. Through centuries of grazing on meager grasses and heather, on kelp that washed in from the sea, he developed into the smallest and most sound pony on earth. Any of his weaker brethren just didn't survive, and the island inhabitants who fished and farmed what good land there was had no intention of supporting weak animals of any sort.

Being small and able to forage for himself, he required little care; being strong, he made a good work horse. He packed great baskets of peat into villages, carried fish from the docks, brought in cartloads of wool for which the islands have long been famous. He was also capable of carry-

Captain Topper, one of the greatest model Shetlands of all time, poses at Pebble Beach, California. He is owned by Miss Patricia Burton of Dryden, Michigan, who paid $56,500 for this golden dapple at public auction in 1958.

ing adults on his brawny back and probably did his share in the preparation and harvest of potatoes, turnips, barley, and oats which the islands have long produced.

For hundreds of years, because of his practicality and because of almost total isolation, the Shetland was kept nearly pure. Today, there are draft horses on the Shetland Islands, but seldom have they been bred to pony blood. Aside from a few Arabian and Icelandic pony crosses in the 1880s, the Shetland can honestly claim one of the longest pure heritages in all of horsedom.

As ties grew between the Shetland Islands and Scotland, many ponies were brought to the mainland where their engaging qualities quickly endeared them to both the Scotch and English. Many of the great castles began breeding them and in 1890 Scottish breeders formed the Shetland

Drinking cool clear water from an Oregon stream is X-Dapples (pronounced Exline Dapples), famous father of Frisco Pete shown on page 41. This superb dappled chestnut with white mane and tail has run barefoot all his life and never been in a show ring, yet has sired some of the best show Shetlands in the country, is owned by Mr. and Mrs. Robert Helms of Grants Pass, Oregon.

Pony Stud Book Society, producing Volume I of its stud book the following year.

In the United States the Shetland seems to have caught on even more ardently, as witness the formation two years earlier of the American Shetland Pony Club in 1888. Mortimer Levering, Eli Elliot, J. Murray Hoag, Robert Lilburn, and Buffalo Bill Cody were among the 205 breeders and owners mentioned in early volumes which interestingly included 29 residents of the Shetland Islands. Mr. Lilburn owned one of the largest herds in the United States and registered over 200 Shetland ponies in 1906, while Mr. Levering, one of the founders of the International Livestock Exhibition in Chicago, was an enthusiastic promoter of the breed.

Today, Canada and the Netherlands have their own Shetland pony stud books, as well as the United States and Britain, and the doughty little Shetland has spread throughout Europe, even to parts of Africa and South America.

The peak of importations to the United States and Canada was in 1906 when more than 425 pedigreed Shetlands were brought over. The pony at that time was always under 11 hands (44 inches); in fact, 46 inches is the height limit in the United States today, and it is even smaller in the British Isles.

In those days our stock resembled the original Islands pony, chunky and heavy-boned, but Americans have always had the habit of improving whatever they adapted to their environment, whether it be an animal, machine, or idea. The Shetland was no exception. For two reasons he underwent a profound change in looks or type. First, in the United States he was strictly an object of pleasure and beauty. To pay his way he had to be as good-looking as possible. Second, many thought that because a pony took up less space than a horse and required less upkeep, he might possibly have wide use in cities as a flashy buggy animal. For this work he had to be a refined and showy little fellow. Unfortunately the bicycle and later the car dimmed these hopes, but the movement to refine the Shetland was already well under way through a process of strict selective breeding.

By carefully choosing stock that had not so thick a neck or ham quarters, but moved with good true action, an animated little steed of real beauty began to be produced perhaps once in every twenty foals. These ponies appeared in model and buggy classes at the great livestock shows across the country and created a sensation. Showing was the way to advertize in those days. When a champion was crowned, the owner sold it to a wealthy city man, then went home, trained and brought out another good pony. Most of the early pony men were horse breeders or livestock dealers. They discovered there was money in the right type of pony, the refined, stylish little jewel kind, and they aimed to produce just that.

Proud of his prizewinning Shetland mare, Silver Sensation, and her foal is John Waugh of Seaton, Illinois, who won a 4-H Grand Championship at the Illinois State Fair. Throughout the country ponies have served as 4-H Club projects.

The Horse Show Monthly in 1909, referring to Mr. Charles E. Bunn of Peoria, Illinois, and his exceptional success in upbreeding ponies, remarked the following:

"He says it is now becoming a well-known fact that we are improving the Shetland in America. In this country he is intended for use as a model and fine harness pony, and in looks must have a beautiful head carried high, set well in a long neck, finishing in well-made shoulders, with perhaps a little more length of leg, and much more style, is just as pure a Shetland, with just as good a disposition, and certainly more pleasing to the eye than the older, imported type. Mr. Bunn has evolved the short-legged, dumpy, rather thick-necked little Shelty into a Bijou horse with the impressive style and sweet conformation, the high carriage of a miniature Vere de Vere, and free, fast action of the most fetching sort, still keeping within the height limit of Shetlands and still retaining the disposition of the breed."

One of the foundation sires of the show Shetland was Tom Thumb, No. 170 in the American Shetland registry and bred directly from stock imported by Robert Lilburn. Just about every registered Shetland alive today carries the blood of Tom Thumb through a son, Prince of Wales, and a daughter, Isabella.

Prince of Wales was the first really standout show Shetland. Foaled in 1891 and purchased by the above Mr. Bunn who owned him all his life, this

39-inch bay pony was undefeated for twelve successive years. At the ripe old age of twenty-six he won first prize for stallion and produce at Madison Square Garden in 1916.

Prince of Wales sired many fine Shetlands, but the most outstanding was Grandee, a 40-inch black stallion considered even better than his illustrious father. Grandee, with a trifle more quality in head and higher and more extravagant action, was defeated but twice in his career and was considered the greatest pony bred to that time.

Other early foundation sires were Trinket 101, Laddie B 6500, McDougal 5697, Tippens 35, Riverdale Brownie 4296, Orloff and his sire, Jap. Jap was sold with his harness mate Jack Frost in 1909 to Alfred Vanderbilt for the then phenomenal price of $3000.

In any discussion of Shetland bloodlines three names inevitably come to the forefront—Larigo, Crescent, and Patton.

One of the most famous Shetlands of all time was a 42-inch black stallion named King Larigo. Bred, owned, and exhibited by George A. Heyl of Washington, Illinois, King won 896 firsts and championships in his twenty-two-year lifetime which began in 1907. A tremendously versatile pony, he was unbeatable in harness combinations and halter classes singly and in groups. In 1915 at the Panama Pacific Exposition in San Francisco he won or aided in winning 72 blue ribbons. In 1917 he was sold to "Diamond Jim" Brady for the astronomical price of $10,000, only to be bought back four years later by the Heyl family. King Larigo sired innumerable great ponies which formed the Larigo line of Shetlands, a byword among Shetland owners today.

Father of the Crescent line of Shetlands is Silver Crescent, a dappled chestnut bred in 1915 by Earl M. Dixon of New Boston, Illinois, and sold for $350 in 1918 to D. G. "Pop" Welty, a school teacher who found he could make a lot more money with Shetlands. "Shorty" as the little dappled chestnut was nicknamed, won a barrel full of ribbons and championships, including some $1000 stakes when they were first inaugurated for ponies back in the mid 1920s. As a sire, he produced many great ponies that have carried the Crescent line to glory.

The Patton line rose from a grandson of Prince of Wales named Black Patton and his son Lyon's Patton. From this blood came Patton L, first Grand National Shetland Champion to be crowned in 1947 and a host of fine show ponies which have distinguished themselves through the years to this day.

What is the modern Shetland conformation? It is best shown by comparing the old with the new where one will see that the head has been refined, particularly around the muzzle. The forehead is wide, the eye prominent and gentle. The nostril is well-formed. The ears are small, alert,

The immortal King Larigo (1907–29), one of the winningest Shetland Ponies of all time and a founder of the modern show Shetland, won championships at all the major state fairs and expositions from coast to coast and in Canada. From age two to sixteen, he garnered 896 firsts and championships and founded the famous Larigo strain of Shetlands. Bred and owned by Heyl Pony Farm of Washington, Illinois, he was once sold to Diamond Jim Brady for $10,000. Note the great leg action of this pony.

Curtis Frisco Pete, one of the great modern Shetlands, six times National Champion, owned by Mr. and Mrs. A. C. Buehler of Fernwood Farms, Barrington, Illinois. The slightly longer legs enhance the graceful body lines in the modern Shetland.

Shetland yearling stallion class at Northwest Shetland Show, Portland, Oregon. Judge W. L. Yount of Iowa on extreme right has just decided in favor of pony on the left, Rock 'n' Roll's Mr. Blitz, trained and shown by Joe Biles of Beaverton, Oregon. Second place pony on right is Flame of Wonder being handled by Roy Jones.

pointed, and well-shaped, giving the head character and quality. A Roman nose amounts to disqualification, and the pony is always shown with full mane and tail.

The throatlatch is narrow and fine. The neck itself is longer and much thinner than in the old days, and it flows gracefully into the pony's body, is never just stuck on the frame like a thick wedge.

The shoulder should have a 45-degree slope and blend smoothly into fine, sharp withers. The barrel is longer than in the old Islands pony, and the back is not so broad and wide, like the near tabletop that Shetlands used to have. The croup is long and carried almost level with the top line (top of the back), and the tail springs high and stylishly from it.

The Shetland's legs are an important part of the change we see today in the pony. They are far more refined than the heavy-boned and heavy-jointed legs of the old Islands type. Also, the legs are a shade longer, particularly above the knees and hocks. Short cannons, both front and rear, still remain but the upper part of the legs has been lengthened and it is this which gives the show Shetland his high, reaching style of action. A pony with short legs cannot lift and reach. His rear legs do not have enough drive. Consequently his front leg action tends to be short and choppy.

All this has not changed the height of the pony, only his proportions. The chubby, blocky look is gone. The muscles and rib cage still show the old iron constitution which has made the Shetland famous. The modern Shelty has an aliveness about him, an animation which immediately attracts attention. He's not a dull fellow at all, but a real little sparkler.

In the matter of action, it is generally agreed that any Shetland with good conformation will usually have good action. Much of this is the result of proper training and shoeing. In recent years however, judging has leaned more and more toward high action, to the point where too often conformation, disposition, pure breeding have been sacrificed to gain this point. Often in fine harness classes the best conformed ponies lost to less handsome ones with extreme action. To meet the competition, some breeders crossed Hackney blood into the Shetland to provide this added point, but as a result conformation and disposition suffered, for Hackneys are far from sweet-mannered. But the real Shetland breeders have stuck by their beliefs and gained their progress by selectivity and not outcrossing. Thus they have maintained the "Shetland look" and good disposition while vastly improving action.

The ideal Shetland action should be high but free and airy, a kind of floating motion as if he were traveling on springs.

Heightwise, the Shetland can never be over 46 inches (11.2 hands), and the true Shetland is smaller than this. Eli Elliot, after a visit to the Shetland Islands to buy and import ponies some seventy years ago, pointed out, "As a rule, they are forty to forty-three, and some as small as thirty-six to thirty-eight inches."

Today the American Shetland is divided into two groups called "Over" and "Under," the former referring to those ponies over forty-three and as high as forty-six inches, the latter to those forty-three inches and under. For many years the dividing line was forty-two inches, but this was raised an inch by popular request in 1963. Nearly fifty percent of the show ponies were forty-two inches on the line and had to have their hoofs cut down every four weeks or so to stay within this height. Also, it helped equalize the size of the two divisions better.

The smaller category of Shetland has tended to be more popular both

Tamerlane's Silver Moon, under 42-inch Shetland Harness Champion, owned by Mr. and Mrs. Joe B. Shelton and sons, Paris, Tennessee. Note the fine action front and back. Front action can be made to some degree by weighted shoeing, but hock action must be born into the pony.

as a show pony and as a pleasure pony. He is more spicy and stylish, and his thimble elegance, when he possesses it, is like nothing else in the horse or pony world. In recent years, however, the taller pony has come into strong demand, particularly as a trotter and roadster.

In 1957 the Shetland height was lowered to forty-four inches, matching the requirements of the British Isles, but there was so much general opposition that it was raised back up to forty-six inches where it now stands.

Shows have played an important role in the rise, change, and growth of the Shetland. In the early days, pony classes were held at the major horse shows and livestock exhibitions across the country. This is still done today, but more and more the all-pony show is appearing on the scene. This has the distinct advantage of bringing all the pony people together

Superb Shetland Pair Class winners at Chicago International are Pierre Coty's Accent and Wildfire, being driven by Ernie Peel for Burnidge Brothers, Elgin, Illinois. Note their brilliant carriage and action, also uniformity of size and color.

for an interesting one- or two-day exhibition and often several breeds contribute to the program, so the public has a good opportunity to see and compare.

The Pekin, Illinois, Pony Show with Shetland and Welsh divisions is held annually on July 3 and 4. Begun in 1963, the show attracted twenty thousand paid admissions the final night which featured the championship stakes of both breeds, a brass band, community bellringing and fireworks.

The American Shetland Pony Club authorizes four types of shows: AA, A, B, and C. The difference lies in the number of classes offered in the program. In an AA show, which is the largest, a minimum of thirty-four events (classes) is required, and several additional classes would probably be included. An A show requires twenty-eight classes, B and C shows less.

In 1964, which was the greatest Shetland show season on record, approximately fifteen hundred Shetland ponies were shown throughout the country in sixty-four A and AA shows comprising the toughest competition.

Shetland shows are separated into two divisions: breeding and performance. This latter principally includes the various harness divisions, both professional and amateur, also a special performance division for children—English and Western equitation, parade and fancy turnout.

A Shetland show always starts with a Model Class. The rule book says, "These classes are to be judged solely on conformation and are designed to set a 'pattern' or 'standard' of ideal Shetland ponies which is to be followed in all other classes for the show." Judging is done 75 percent on conformation and 25 percent on character and quality.

The Breeding or "In-Hand" Class Shetlands are judged 60 percent on conformation and 40 percent on performance, quality, and manners.

Group classes such as Get of Sire (three Shetlands of any sex from the same sire 46" and under) or Herd of Four (one stallion and three mares of any age, 46" and under, one owner) are judged 75 percent on conformation and 25 percent on uniformity and are not to be worked.

In Single Harness Shetland Classes as well as pairs, tandem, unicorns (three ponies hitched as two wheelers and one lead) and combination ponies (ride and drive) all entries are driven to a viceroy, side bar buggy or four-wheeled vehicle of similar type.

Single Harness Shetlands are judged 40 percent on conformation and 60 percent on performance, quality, and manners. Excessive speed is considered undesirable. The same rules apply to most of the group harness Shetlands.

The Roadster Class for Shetlands was begun in 1951 and has turned into a most popular event. The entrants are driven to a sulky, bike, or two-wheeled vehicle of similar type. Judging is done 20 percent on conformation and quality, 20 percent on manners and way of going, described as free motion and extended trot, and 60 percent on speed in form. Drivers must wear racing colors (silk caps and jackets—stable colors preferred).

The Saddle and Parade Pony classes are for children under fourteen and are conducted under American Horse Show Association rules.

One of the most beautiful of children's classes is the Fancy Turnout. A girl and a boy, neither over twelve, ride side by side in a buggy, the boy driving, the girl holding flowers. If it is an evening class, the girl wears a formal evening dress that falls over hoops surrounding the buggy, the boy sports tails and a top hat. The class is judged 50 percent on the children's attire, 40 percent on conformation, manners, and performance of the pony and 10 percent on neatness and cleanliness of the harness and vehicle.

In Portland, Oregon, youthful driver Jane Helms wins the Shetland Fine Harness Class with her Butterfly's Showboy and is presented trophy by Rose Festival Queen.

Ladies' Driving Class, both singles and pairs, are also popular among the distaff as well as with the crowd. They are judged 40 percent on conformation and 60 percent on manners, quality, and performance. Uniformity and similarity of action are also considered in pairs.

Each win at a recognized Shetland show gives a pony a certain number of points toward an annual All Star rating. An AA or A show win provides more points than a similar win at a B or C show. At the end of the year the

Roadster ponies have become tremendously popular in the last decade. In the show ring they have three gaits, the jog, trot or road-gait, and turn-on which is a racing trot. Shown here is Grey Flash being driven in a Lady's Roadster Class at the turn-on gait by Mrs. George Litchfield of Bartlett, Illinois.

American Shetland Pony Club totals up and announces the winners in its monthly *Journal,* and owners are justly proud of this recognition. Of the awards, the club says:

"The National Shetland All-Stars are, in effect, the best Shetlands being shown today; however, their rankings do not reflect any attempt to judge their relative merits, or any individual preferences. These rankings are, instead, based on the results of their placings at the shows, both large and small, and thus reward not only excellent performance but also frequency of competition."

One of the great sources of strength for the Shetland has been the American Shetland Pony Club. Organized in 1888, it has kept the breed alive during its lean years in the 1930s and 40s, and has done its best to regulate and control the fantastic growth of the Shetland since 1950. It is older than any horse club or registry we have today, older than the sacred Jockey Club which registers the racing Thoroughbred.

The ASPC, as it is called, boasts a membership of nearly 7500, from all

A most popular children's class is the Fancy Turnout in which pony, vehicle, boy and his girl dress their best. Shown here are Mr. Spatz and Stephen and Georgette Litchfield of Bartlett, Illinois, All-American Champions, 1961–2–3–4.

our states and Canada. Since 1888 it has registered almost 115,000 Shetlands, approximately 80 percent of which have been recorded since 1946. There is estimated to be between 45,000 and 50,000 registered Shetlands in the United States and Canada today. Annual registry of new ponies amounts to about 6000 and many times that number are transferred to new owners.

The club has done much to promote the Shetland. One of its pet projects has been an annual National Breed Promotion Sale. Begun in 1946 and held each fall, it has netted the club a considerable profit which has aided in further promoting the breed. The average price in that first sale was $285 per head. In 1957 it reached an all-time high of $2379 per head. Shetland prices have dropped since then, but there are many healthy signs indicative of prices returning, especially as the pony is put to wider use.

The club also sponsors the National Shetland Pony Congress. Held in 1964 at Des Moines in conjunction with the Iowa State Fair, this World

Series of Shetland ponies had over $8500 in premiums including two $1000 championship fine harness stakes.

Other important functions of the club are the organizing and conducting of judging clinics, training clinics, and the like. These highly informative discussion groups, led by authorities and trainers, have supplied considerable basic knowledge to newcomers and youngsters, and have brought more uniformity to Shetland judging.

The Shetland Futurity is another project of the club. Between 800 and 1000 mares are nominated annually and the foals which are born to them share in almost $10,000 worth of prize money when they grow up— and if they are good enough to win.

The club has also been instrumental in helping 4-H Club pony projects across the country. In these most worthwhile ways the energy of our American youth is channeled into wholesome recreational pursuit. Knowledge, experience, and a sense of values are all developed. More of 4-H Club pony projects and how to organize one later.

The club maintains headquarters at Lafayette, Indiana, and publishes a very fine breed magazine called *The American Shetland Pony Journal* at Aledo, Illinois.

In 1964 the United States Pony Trotting Associaton became affiliated as a separate corporation with the American Shetland Pony Club. The latter keeps records, issues Eligibility Certificates and devotes a section of the *Journal* to pony racing. On its own, the club promotes a National

A fine matched team of pulling Shetlands heave into their collars and traces to move a heavy load of cement blocks. They are owned by Robert Foster of Amanda, Ohio.

Championship Stake Race each year, and it currently carries a purse of around $15,000. At this time about twenty percent of the trotting ponies which are being raced are registered Shetlands.

Another interesting aspect of the Shetland world is pony pulling. In the old days at fairs and horse shows, great teams of Percherons, Belgians, and Shires had pulling contests to see which could drag the heaviest amount of weight. But since these giant draft horses have just about left the American farm scene, the sport of pony pulling has risen with amazing popularity in recent years to take its place. Ponies are much more easily kept and transported than huge draft horses, and they provide just as much fun and excitement. When they lean into the traces and move a heavy load forward, they are just as overawing as a pair of mammoth Shires. Today they appear at many fairs and livestock exhibitions in the country, particularly the Midwest. Thus the American Shetland Pony Club has recommended the following rules for Shetland Pony Pulling Matches:

GENERAL RULES

1. Classes open for registration and/or grade Shetland ponies.
2. No pony is to measure over 46" (including shoes).
3. All matches are to be pulled on percentage of weight not overweight. For example a team of ponies weighing 600 pounds and pulling on 150 percent of their weight would be pulling 900 pounds. 200 percent equals 1200 pounds; 300 percent equals 1800 pounds.
4. Ponies must be weighed before each contest; weights of previous matches will not be accepted.
5. Only one driver allowed per team; the man doing the hooking must not encourage the ponies in any way.

PULLING-MATCH RULES

6. The sled will be loaded with weighed weights, preferably cement or salt blocks.
7. The doubletrees will be hooked to a twelve-foot cable which pulls under a shive, which is staked to the ground. This will make the sled travel the same track.
8. Each team will be given three pulls with a three-minute limit per pull to slide the sled six feet.
9. There shall be two judges; one who checks the distance of the pulls, and one who judges the driver and determines when he completes a pull.
10. The doubletrees must clear the ground before the team fall into their collars; this eliminates bumping the load to start it.

11. In cases where breakdowns occur, the driver has the privilege of counting or rejecting the pull.
12. A pull is completed any time the doubletrees touch the ground after the ponies have raised them free of the ground.
13. After the team completes its tries, the sled is pulled back to the starting position with a tractor and loaded for the next team.

DISQUALIFICATION

14. The driver and team will be disqualified from the contest if the driver should strike or whip his team with the end of the line.
15. No whips of any kind are permitted in the ring.
16. Abuse of ponies inside the pulling arena disqualifies a driver from the contest.

As mentioned in the first chapter, Shetlands have begun to play a key role in the field of training mentally retarded and delinquent children. Some outstanding pioneering in this field has been done by Mr. and Mrs. Charles Wheeler of Rankin, Illinois. Both have degrees in Psychology and have studied under Dr. Samuel Kirk, leading U.S. authority on mentally retarded children and the only American recipient of the first awards of the Joseph P. Kennedy, Jr., Foundation, given in 1962 to researchers for outstanding achievements in the field of mental retardation.

Dr. Kirk helped the Wheelers formulate their home for mentally retarded children on a farm near Rankin. The original nine youngsters progressed so outstandingly through a system of using the Shetland to learn both academically and of life in general that the Wheelers' method became recognized as a new and valuable approach to an old problem.

To bring a mentally retarded child up to the third or fourth grade level takes up to ten years. Until the Wheelers developed their pony affiliation method, such children, which number about two percent of our juvenile population, were confined to institutions or hidden away in attics.

Now, Children's House in Carmel Valley, California, is using Shetlands in the Wheeler manner, and Miss Patricia Burton of Dryden, Michigan, is setting up a Children's Village project in this field. After Dr. Kirk completes his studies and the Wheeler method becomes more widely known, children's homes throughout the world will probably change their training and refocus educational systems around the Shetland pony and a child's natural love for it.

In Norway, Shetlands have been used most successfully in rehabilitating polio-stricken children. Doctors report that spastic cases remain more mobile after short rides, even short walks, on ponies. The ponies are also used abroad for accident patients recovering from leg and back injuries.

The ride provides healthy use of all muscles, and association with the animal has great therapeutic value mentally.

More than two-thirds of the Shetlands in the United States today are of "grade" type, that is, without registration papers or pedigree to show their breeding. They number probably around a 100,000 and many possess excellent conformation and ability. But because a previous owner neglected to register an ancestor, or perhaps a parent or grandparent was of grade or even imported stock (the modern American Shetland is today so different from the Shetland Islands type that imports are no longer accepted for registry here), the pony has no all-important "papers." Thus in 1952 the Shetland Pony Identification Bureau was organized by Mrs. Beatrice Langfeld of Omaha, Nebraska, to undertake the registration of these grade Shetlands after they had passed inspection. It's now incorrect to say that all grade ponies are unregistered. Many have papers from SPIB and several shows in various parts of the country hold classes for them.

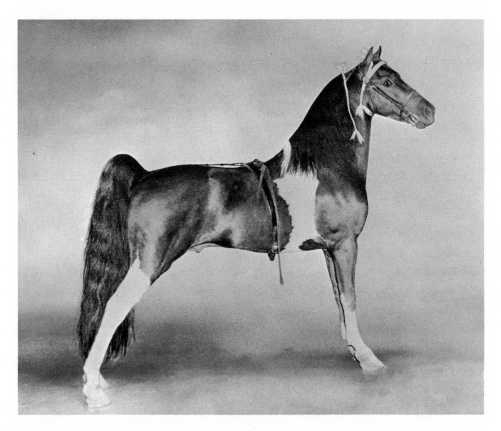

Beauty in every line—this is what the modern pinto show Shetland has evolved into. Shown here in a model pose is Heatherstone Bugle Call, owned by Silverstone Farm, Sheboygan Falls, Wisconsin.

The Shetland pony has passed through several eras here in America. First was the Islands or Imported type; then came refinement of that chunky little fellow into a prettier, more snappy and alert pony. Then in the 1950s people began to buy "color"; the startling silver and golden dapples and beautifully refined pintos became the rage. At the moment the show Shetland is in an "action" era where extreme elevation is the last word.

But come what may, he will continue on his good-natured way, keeping his iron constitution and friendly disposition, bringing fun and pleasure in a multitude of ways to children and adults by the thousands as he always has. For this is what has made him the most popular pony in the world.

Chapter 3

The Hackney

For good reason the Hackney has been called the Prince of Ponies. Of all the breeds and varieties of horses, none typifies elegance quite as much as does this little firebrand. His closest rivals are probably the five-gaited American Saddlebred and the Hackney horse, both masters of beauty, grace, and poise. Yet by their very size they lack those fascinating qualities which diminutive members of a species, even people, always have—the complete self-assurance, the reckless vivacity, the saucy zest for living. Horsemen call this temperament the "pony character" and in the Hackney it reaches its zenith.

This dancing extremist is not considered a very versatile performer. He can trot as fast as the best of ponies, but he does not lower himself to the bawdiness of a roadster class or a trotting race, although a few of his more daft brethren have slipped surreptitiously and successfully into these leagues. He is never jumped, though his half-brother, the Hackney horse, has broken world's jumping records. He is almost never ridden, except (don't tell anybody) in parade pony classes where he prances along at a teeth-rattling parade gait that no other competitor can match in showiness.

No, he is a specialist, bred 150 years ago in England to be only a harness pony of the highest caliber, and continued improvement has left him without a peer. He draws a viceroy (a four-wheeled light carriage) polished to the gleam of a black diamond. He is driven by a man in a sedately proper business suit and bowler or by a woman in evening attire. He has but two gaits, a park pace and a smart trot. Only in movements abandoned to pasture leisure does he walk or gallop.

All this would seem to describe a rather dull and stuffy animal, which the Hackney most certainly is not. He is a pony for adults only. His training requires patience and knowledge for full development. It is expensive, and if he makes the grade he becomes a valuable hunk of horseflesh running up into the thousands of dollars.

The history of the Hackney pony is the history of the Hackney horse, one that dates back to the time of William Langland, who in the second

Creation's King, world's leading Hackney pony sire for twelve consecutive years (1951–63), displays the form and action that have made the breed famous. This brilliant grandson of the immortal King of the Plain is owned by Kennedy Pony Farm, Taylorville, Illinois.

half of the fourteenth century said in *The Vision Concerning Piers Plowman:* "Ac hakeneyes hadde thei none, bote hakeneyes to hyre."

This does not refer to the breed of horse as we think of him today, but rather to a type of horse that was used for hacking along roads.

No doubt the Romans helped improve the British equine stock, which was probably of pony height when they arrived. Later the Danes or Norsefolk who invaded and settled at Norfolk, brought with them horses of dun, sorrel, and chestnut whose best gait was the trot.

Through the centuries the terms Hackney and Roadster were applied to these horses of the road, whether under saddle or driven, which stood over fourteen hands. Norfolk and Yorkshire led in the production of these animals. The Norfolk trotters became world famous and the finest early Thoroughbred blood, that of the Darley Arabian through Flying Childers, Blaze, and Shales, was crossed into this blood. In colonial America this

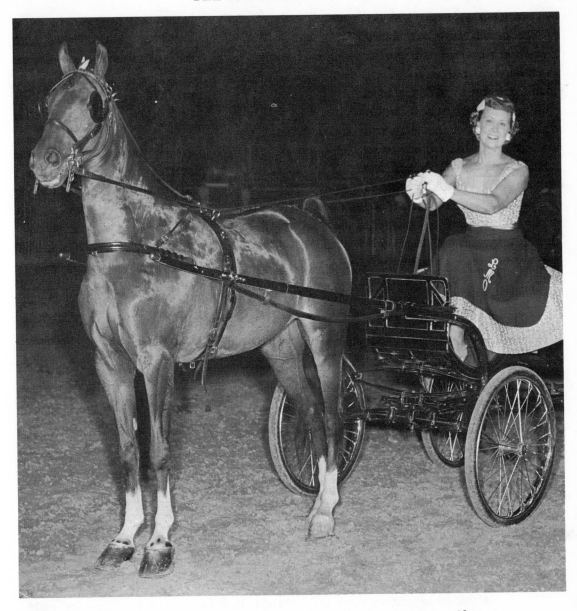

Winning a Ladies Class is Queen of Banner being driven by Mrs. L. Marion Oliver of Berea, Kentucky. This 12.1 hand Hackney mare is sired by the famous King of Belgium.

blood produced our early Narragansett Pacers and later the famous Canadian Pacers, forerunners of our modern Standardbred.

In eighteenth-century England the country roads were abominable. While stagecoaches, hauled by giant horses, made the trek from city to city, light buggies could not. Thus a horse under saddle became the means of individual travel, and for this the Hackney was the most popular because of his fine trot. Naturally Norfolk and Yorkshire led in the production of these animals.

As city streets improved, there rose a demand for a high-class carriage horse, a trotter of strength and elegance. At this point the Hackney was put to harness and has never been equaled in this capacity since.

The Hackney pony in its early stages was not distinguished from his larger brother. They were just different-sized Hackneys. In fact, many of the early Hackneys were on the small side because the majority of the English horses were small.

The Hackney pony was stabilized into a breed by a few men who deliberately set out to do so. They gathered up the best small Hackneys they could find and began line-breeding to set the blood.

Mr. Christopher Wilson of Kirby Lonsdale, Westmorland, using the bloodlines of D'Oyley's Confidence and Lord Derby 2nd, two famous Hackneys of the 1860s, produced Sir Horace who proved the greatest pony sire of his day.

About this same time Mr. C. E. Cooke of Litcham, Norfolk, produced Cassius, a grandson of Lord Derby 2nd and another outstanding Hackney Pony winner and producer. His two sons, Julius Caesar 2nd and Whitegate Swell, proved great sires, the former creating the Torchfire line of great steppers, the blood of which is still seen today in some American ponies.

The Berkeley Stud, owned by Mr. R. Day, became famous mainly through a great Hackney pony, Berkeley Model, who in 1895 at the London Hackney Show bested Sir Horace for the only defeat of his career. Berkeley Model sired several outstanding ponies and one of his sons produced Southworth Swell, famous champion of the 1920s.

The Melbourne Stud of Mr. Walter Cliff and the Tissington Stud of Sir Gilbert Greenall also produced outstanding Hackney ponies, both employing the Confidence and Sir Horace lines.

The English Hackney Stud Book Society was formed in 1883 for the purpose of registering and keeping a stud book for "Hackneys, Roadsters, Cobs and Ponies." Stud records had been kept privately for many years prior to this, but as carriage shows became more popular, there came the need to classify and create a breed. Actually, "Hackney" was still a term applied to any high stepper, and often Welsh or other blood that had the high, airy motion entered into the competition. With the creation of a Hackney Society, the high stepper became solidified into today's breed.

The American Hackney Horse Society was founded with 228 members in 1891. Its first Stud Book appeared in 1893. As the name indicates, the original intent was to register Hackney horses which were at their peak of popularity at that time. As this breed waned, the Hackney pony took its place and today comprises 95 percent of the registry.

Bellfounder (Jary's No. 55) was the first known Hackney to be brought
to this country, in 1822. A renowned trotter, this fifteen-hand bay stallion
helped found the Standardbred and was the maternal grandsire of Hambletonian. Thus his claim to fame lies more in this direction than through
any Hackney pony line.

In the 1870s and 1880s many fine Hackneys were brought to this country,
but the records generally listed them as horses regardless of their size.
Many were small, like fourteen-hand Little Wonder, hit of the 1883 Madison Square Garden Show and imported by Mr. A. J. Cassatt of Philadelphia, first president of the society. Another pony of brilliant action was

*A harness Pony Class at Devon Horse Show is dominated by long-tail Hackney
ponies of 12.2 hands and under. A "header" stands in front of each pony after
line-up. They are judged on manners, quality, and performance.*

Fashion, a son of old Confidence and imported by Mr. Prescott Lawrence. He proved the sensation of the Boston, New York, and Philadelphia shows and fired up much of the interest that led to mass importations in the late 1880s and 1890s.

In 1903 Mr. W. D. Henry brought over Enfield Nipper and Dilham Prime Minister (¼ Thoroughbred), considered the two foundation sires of the modern American Hackney pony.

Each succeeding year more and more Hackneys were imported, always the best because this was a rich man's sport equivalent to our sportscar enthusiasts of today. The imported ponies inevitably ran off with all the ribbons. America seemed unable to produce the brilliant Hackneys of the English though they used the same blood. This became a challenge to many men, one of whom was Mr. J. Macy Willets. At his Cassilis Farm in New Marlboro, Massachusetts, he assembled some great Hackney blood and began in earnest to breed the snappy little pony in American style. His first sire, Irvington Autocrat by Dilham Prime Minister, provided a worthy start, but his true success came in 1925 when he imported Southworth Swell. This was the greatest sire of Hackney ponies in England during the 1920s, and so he proved to be here.

America now began in earnest to produce high quality Hackneys, but there remained one more great star to be imported—King of the Plain. This is possibly the greatest Hackney of all time, certainly the most influential Hackney ever to stomp American tanbark.

King of the Plain, an in-bred descendant of Sir Horace, was bought as a two-year-old in 1927 by Bertram Mills, an agent acting for J. R. Thompson of Chicago. It is doubtful that the seller realized how great a young pony he had, for the following year the fine trainer Harold Jenkinson brought him out in harness and won the championship stakes at Toronto and Chicago, a near miraculous feat for a three-year-old.

For the next ten years this sensational pony was invincible. The only other pony of that day who might have bested him was Billet Doux, but this beautiful mare died tragically in a barn fire at Oakland, California, before they ever met. In 1935 Miss Frances Dodge, owner of the famed Meadowbrook Farm, purchased King of the Plain, and for the Dodge Stables he produced many outstanding champions.

Highland Cora, Highland Magic, King's Banner, King of the Highlands, and many other high-stepping winners proved of such superior quality that the blood of King of the Plain today literally dominates almost every Hackney show pony pedigree in America. This stallion has been to the Hackney what Hambletonian was to the Standardbred and King to the Quarter horses. His blood is still just as potent as ever, though promulgated now by grandchildren and great-grandchildren. Any Hackney with the

A beautiful tandem performance shows both Hackneys in cadence. Traces between ponies should be slack, not taut; vehicle is a gig. They are owned by George H. Griffiths of Cedar Rapids, Iowa.

Hackneys are showy ponies, always dark in color, often with white socks. Here youthful amateur handler Douglas Oliver of Berea, Kentucky, beats the professionals with a beautiful mare.

word King in his name is surely a descendant of this all-time great high-stepper.

The Hackney registry annually records some eight hundred to a thousand new ponies, and transfers to new owners amount to about the same. In the early days the East was the stronghold for the Hackney, but in recent years the Midwest, California, and the South have had great growth among his followers. Canada has long been a lover of this little fireball as well as his larger counterpart, the Hackney horse. Canada has its own society and registry. Transfer of records from one country to the other is constant, and shows both sides of the border are strongly attended by each group. From Canadian stables have come some of the outstanding winners at U.S. shows, including Devon. The extensive Hackney program at this, the largest outdoor horse show in the country, is considered equivalent to a Hackney National if one were to be held, which will probably be the case in the not too distant future.

In looks, the Hackney is a neat, clean, and very alert pony. His eye is bold and prominent, ears small and popped forward intensely. Though his muzzle and head are refined, he nearly always has a Roman nose. His neck is on the long side, never thick but refined and the crest shows clearly, particularly under harness when the head is tucked. The neck flows into a fine sloping shoulder and sturdy chest. Withers on a good Hackney are never prominent. The rib cage is well sprung, the fore and hind quarters on the squarish and muscular side but never coarse in a draft horse way. The leg bone is good and solid but not heavy, for the Hackney pony is the anthesis of refinement without weakness. His walk is quick and springy, his trot is high and airy, sharp and true. All his actions are nimble and spritely, never ponderous like those of a horse, and he bubbles with energy.

The predominant color of Hackney ponies is bay. A few come in brown or black. Just about all other colors have been bred out of them. They often sport white socks or stockings and white head markings. In height they generally range from twelve to fourteen hands, though an occasional one comes along a shade over or under this.

For showing, the Hackney pony is divided into two groups, the Cob-Tail and the Long-Tail. The Cob-Tail was the original type brought over from England and so named because its tail was docked to a six-inch nubbin for distinctive carriage style. Though some states bar this operation today on the grounds of cruelty, the practice, like that of altering dogs' ears and tails, remains widespread mainly because it is traditionally the way the Hackney is turned out. The pony's mane is also tightly braided when he is shown in this style. The Cob-Tail division is divided into two height classifications—over 13.0 hands, and 13.0 hands and under.

Hackney pony gets his tail unwrapped and a last-minute brush before entering show ring at Devon, Pennsylvania. Note the elaborate stallion tack which keeps the pony's head tucked, neck arched, and tail high.

The Long-Tail is an interesting and relatively new offshoot of the Hackney pony. In the late 1940s a group got together and began crossing the Hackney with the Shetland to create what they called the Harness pony. This Harness pony, intended to be a jazzed-up Shetland or a smaller, more refined Hackney, was to be shown with a long flowing mane and tail, in fine harness and viceroy, and he was to be the epitome of all other harness ponies in style and beauty. The cross was made, the height limited to 12.2 hands and under, and Harness pony classes began to spring up at all the major shows. The fly in the soup proved to be that the classes were not restricted to this crossbred pony but open to anyone who dared

compete against him. Soon the people with small Hackneys stopped bob-
tailing them. In a short time Harness pony classes were swamped with
snappy little Hackneys with long flowing manes and tails. Their action
was so brilliant that they drove out everyone else and today they have
this classification all to themselves. Though the door is still open for any
breed to enter, no one beats them at this, their forte.

Thus today the Hackney pony comes in two styles—the Cob-Tail with
the nubbin of a tail and braided mane, and the Long-Tail with a fly-
swisher that flows to the ground and a mane that flutters like a flag when
he turns on the speed.

Like nearly all pony groups these days, the Hackney Society conducts
an annual futurity designed to encourage breeders to produce the best
possible results from their breeding programs. A futurity is a progessive-
payment money stake. If you think you can breed a good pony, you pay
the initial nomination fee. If you produce a good foal, you pay the entry
fee. If you win, you get a good bundle of greenbacks.

*Little Gypsy, queen of the Florida Sunshine Circuit of horse shows, is shown being
driven by Lloyd Teater for owners Mr. and Mrs. John A. Snively, Jr., of Winter
Haven, Florida.*

The Hackney Pony Futurity is held each year at the Devon Horse Show. It consists of four divisions, yearling, two-year-old, three-year-old Short-Tail (Cob), and three-year-old Long-Tail. The major rules, in a somewhat condensed form, are as follows:

A — All foals must be nominated by April 1 in the year in which they become yearlings. Fee: $10. To be shown in hand.

B — The sire must be nominated at the same time. Fee: $10.

C — All two-year-olds must be nominated by April 1 in the year in which they become two-year-olds. Fee: $10. If they were not nominated as yearlings a double fee will be charged. To be shown in hand.

D — All three-year-olds must be nominated by April 1 in the year in which they become three-year-olds. Fee: $10. To be shown in harness with short mane and tail.

E — All three-year-olds must be nominated by April 1 in the year in which they become three-year-olds. Fee: $10. To be shown in harness with long mane and tail, and pony not to be over fifty inches in height.

In addition to the fees received, the American Hackney Horse Society contributes $500 to be divided between the four divisions. The prize money for each division is divided 50 percent for first, 20 percent for second. 15 percent for third, 10 percent for fourth and 5 percent for fifth. From the $10 fees at every turn, it is easy to see how the pot builds up and interest stimulates among all breeders.

Though Hackneys are among the most pampered animals on earth, they're no frail little bundles of flim-flam, but tough ponies with boundless courage and spirit. Their job is not an easy one. It demands endless training and precision. Proper harnessing and shoeing play a key roll in their success. In personality and temperament, the Hackney pony is frisky, high-strung and very intelligent. You don't fight him, otherwise you'll be fighting him the rest of your life. He's a sensitive gamin, likes company, loves to put on a show, and he's generally too spirited to be a child's pet. Adults made him as a showpiece for themselves and they are the ones who love him.

What is the thrill of the Hackney?

In part, it's the brilliance of the pony and his way of going, full of dash, poise, balance, rhythm. In part, it's the skill of driving such a little fireball to bring out this magnificent action, the thrill of collecting him and keeping him in his precision, of restraint yet freedom, for you cannot heave and haul on a Hackney's mouth and get far with him.

Top Flight, a long-tail West Coast Hackney star, shows the magnificent form and style of his illustrious grandfather, King of the Plain. Owner is Mr. William P. Roth of San Mateo, California.

In part, it's the thrill of turning out the pony and vehicle in all its miniature splendor—of washing the pony's white socks, of grooming his coat to an iridescent gleam, of carefully braiding his mane into fourteen tight little plaits and combing his cob tail into its fiery flag, of polishing the harness and buffing the viceroy, then harnessing up the fiery little steed quivering with excitement, and climbing into the driver's seat in exactly the proper way so the pony is contained. It's moving him out, feeling always the ball of energy on the end of the reins, warming him up and bringing out his best action in regular cadence. It's the competition itself, of manipulating around the other ponies while always maintaining the full spirit and elegance of yours. For the advanced amateur, it is also the thrill of driving a pair and, above all, a tandem in perfect unison, using all the knacks of great driving to show the ponies at their best. In part, it's also living in the past, in the days when life was more leisurely, perhaps more sensible, certainly more elegant.

Only the Hackney could supply all this, which accounts for his survival in our coldly analytical and scientific world of today. He had his lean years in the 1930s and 1940s when he faded almost out of sight, but he has made a startling comeback, to the point where his popularity is now surging across the country. Whether his followers be gnarled-fingered old horsemen or the new group of doctors, lawyers, and the like, to those who know him he remains the Prince of Ponies.

The Welsh can do most anything and kids can do most anything with the Welsh. Here little Janet Van Zandt of Philadelphia rides Gwynedd Jamboree sidesaddle.

Chapter 4
The Welsh

One of the hardiest, most beautiful, and proudest in heritage of all our ponies is the Welsh. Two thousand years ago he carried Britons in war chariots against invading Roman legions with such strength and boldness that Caesar had many of his kind sent back to Rome. The stubborn Briton from Wales never surrendered to the Romans but withdrew to the wild mountains of southwest England where he and his sturdy little horse remained in defiant isolation for centuries.

Thus arose the name Welsh mountain pony, descriptive of this thrifty little fellow, sure-footed as a goat, used for shepherding in rough country, pit mining, carrying loads or full-grown men. Many call him a miniature Arabian for the strong resemblance he often bears to this Eastern breed, but he is more himself—kind, friendly, intelligent, and just about the most versatile of any pony or horse we have today.

An outstanding junior hunter and jumper, he is widely used for pleasure riding both English and Western style, gymkhana, parade and costume events and trail-riding competitions by children seven to fourteen years of age. In the show ring, adults exhibit him in model classes, formal driving, fine harness, and roadster classes, and whole families use him as a sharp racing pony. You name it and the Welsh will do it.

A novice entering the Welsh world for the first time is liable to become confused when confronted by such terms as Welsh mountain pony, Welsh pony, Section B, Welsh Cob, etc.

"Is there a difference in all these?" he will ask.

Yes, there is, but to understand the Welsh, we must first look at him in his native Wales, then here in America. In his homeland the original Welsh was a pony averaging twelve hands and under, of keen intelligence and fine disposition. For centuries herds of Welsh ponies were kept in various mountainous sections, a group of mares with a stallion. Each fall the bands would be rounded up, the foals weaned, some sold, some gelded, some traded, others trained by their various owners who contributed mares to the herd.

Section B Welsh mare and foal owned by Mr. and Mrs. Bohn C. Lindemann, Maidens, Virginia.

During the winter a few might be turned out with a band of sheep, for as they pawed through the snow to the grass and heather, they uncovered food for the sheep. But usually the herds of Welsh ponies were kept in or near towns through the winter, then driven to the mountains in the spring to run free and breed again. Naturally, if the daughters of a stallion were constantly put back into the herd, the stock soon became too closely inbred. Outcrossing could be done either by adding outside mares to a herd or by changing the stallion.

During the eighteenth and nineteenth centuries Arabian, Thoroughbred, and Hackney blood was infused in this manner to upgrade the centuries-old and rather inbred Welsh mountain pony. Arabian blood, having been the most influential, shows today in the characteristics of the head and tail carriage, and in the Welsh's spirit and gait. The other blood shows up in height and body proportions, which is why the Welsh registry is divided into four sections.

Susan McConnell of Greenville, Delaware, takes her high-score Welsh jumping pony, Bray's Island Blue Violet, for a sleigh ride.

Formed in Breconshire in 1898, the Welsh Pony and Cob Society brought out its first stud volume in 1900, categorizing the Welsh into Sections A, B, C, and D. Section A is the original Welsh mountain pony, 12 hands or under in the British Isles, 12.2 hands or under in the United States.

If a pony happens to grow over the height limits of Section A, he is automatically transferred to Section B of the Welsh registry. Height requirements are anything over 12 to 13.2 hands in the English registry, over 12.2 to 14 hands in the American registry. The Section B pony shows the results of outcrossing more than does his smaller brother and is used mostly as a hunter and jumper. In England the term Welsh mountain pony refers only to Section A, the term Welsh pony only to Section B. In America the terms are used interchangeably, distinction being made by reference to specific Sections.

Section C of the Welsh registry in the British Isles is for the Welsh

Cob. This burly little fellow was produced by crossing the original small Welsh mountain pony with draft horse blood to obtain a chunkier, more draft-like animal for the pits and mines of Wales. In height he stands 13.2 or under and is today a popular hunting pony for ladies and larger children in England.

Section D of the Welsh registry in the British Isles is merely for a larger version of the Welsh Cob. He ranges from 13.2 hands on up to 14 and 15 hands, even higher.

The Welsh registry in America does not have a Section C and D at this time. The few Welsh Cobs in the United States today carry only English registry. But it was not always so.

The original registry here was begun in 1906 by the formation of the Welsh Pony and Cob Society of America, incorporated in Illinois. The Shetland far outnumbered the Welsh in those days, but several pony men in the Indiana-Ohio-Illinois area took a fancy to the Welsh during the 1880s and 1890s. Importations were made. Interest spread from Kentucky and Virginia to New England. For showing, members of the Society turned out a "fitted" pony along the lines of the Shetland, and this was the method followed through the years. But interest in the Welsh waned through the 1930s until, by 1943, his ranks had withered to the point where new registrations averaged only six or seven per year, so the Society was dissolved.

In 1946 a reorganization took place with the forming of the Welsh Pony Society of America. The word "Cob," along with the C and D Sections, was dropped because no cobs had ever been registered, also because it was felt that the Cob size and type were too different from that of the pony.

The new club during its first year recorded seventeen registrations, but soon things began to boom. A new group of breeders centered mainly in the Virginia-Maryland-Pennsylvania area made several major importations. Almost immediately New England and the West Coast became involved. Within ten years registrations reached 1500 annually, are currently up to 2000, and well over 10,000 registered Welsh ponies of Section A and Section B type are now spread across every state in our land.

The Welsh Pony Society, located at Unionville, Pennsylvania, divides the United States and Canada into twenty areas, within which regional champions are crowned. These are encouraged to attend the Welsh National Show held each July usually at Devon, Pennsylvania. Here the cream of the Welshes in North America come to compete.

In physical appearance the Welsh exudes boldness and refinement from a body of good muscle and bone. His head, wide between bold eyes, tapers down to a clean, finely-cut muzzle, and is slightly dished, never Roman-nosed. His ears are small, alertly pointed and well-shaped; neck

Linda Donaldson is shown above with her Welsh pony, Coed Coch Seren Lwyd, hitched to cart and below in same class with the same pony under saddle.

The Welsh is a fine jumping pony. Miss Linda Butler takes Gwynedd Jumble over timber with height and style to spare. Owner is Miss Violet Haines of Gwynedd Valley, Pennsylvania.

on the long side, moderately lean in the case of mares, inclined to be cresty in matured stallions. Back is strong and muscular, withers prominent but not knifey, shoulders well developed with a good slope, and good strong legs set well under the pony.

The coat of the Welsh is soft and silky, never coarse, his mane, forelock, and tail are very full and rich, characteristics that owners exclaim so proudly about. The Welsh pony usually has some long hair on the fetlocks. For showing in a model class this need not be clipped, although in the more formal harness and hunter classes it is removed.

In color the Welsh can be anything except piebald and skewbald. He comes in bay, brown, black, dun, chestnut, palomino, gray, and roan. In darker colors he often has white leg or head markings.

Certainly the most frequent color seen in the Welsh is gray. This is said to have come, first, from his Arabian blood and, second, because British breeders in the last fifty years have deliberately bred to obtain this color. With good justification too, for the gray Welsh with full mane and tail flowing in every movement is a beautiful sight. Most gray Welshes are born black, bay, sand, chestnut, or the like, then after a few weeks as

The versatility of the Welsh is shown again in these photos of Imported Stoatley Acorn. Above the mare is hitched to a doctor's gig in a costume class and going in true "floating" style of the Welsh; below she is shown in high action winning a Roadster Class. Owner is Mrs. David Wells of Santa Barbara, California, who is driving in both cases.

the foal coat begins to shed around the eyes and nostrils, a very dark iron-gray appears. As the pony matures, his coat becomes progressively lighter until in later years it is almost white, especially in the case of mares.

The action of the Welsh is, to me, a thing of beauty. The walk and canter are the same as in other ponies, but the trot is a floating glide known to the trade as "daisy cutting." Instead of pulling his legs upward in Hackney fashion, he throws them forward from the shoulder straight and low, and any daisies four to six inches above the ground would be cut off by his low-flying hoofs. When done properly, this floating trot covers a lot of ground, and a crowd always bursts out with "Oh!" and "Ah!" in sheer delight because it's so spectacularly different from all other pony gaits.

In personality the Welsh is a gay blade with a sense of responsibility. He likes to whinny to the mares at a show while carrying his tail with swishing pride. As a worker, he learns quickly, is tractable and gentle around children, not given to nipping and kicking. Endurance and soundness have been his hallmark for centuries, also his ability to forage. A good pasture and a simple shelter are his main requirements, also water, salt, and some hay in the winter if pasture is not available. Grain or mixed feed is recommended for foals during the first winter. Shoes are not necessary for the Welsh unless he is being ridden on hard roads, but his feet should be examined regularly, kept trimmed and straight.

One of the founders of the modern Welsh was a stylish gray pony called Dyoll Starlight, born in 1894 and owned by Mr. Howard Meuric Lloyd of South Wales. Moonlight, his mother, is described as a "miniature Arab full of quality with a lovely head and good shoulder," and was probably descended from the Crawshap Bailey Arab used as a herd stallion in the Brecon Beacons area around 1850. Dyoll Starlight, a gay, free mover, won at the Royal Show from 1898 to 1901, and thereafter his children and grandchildren dominated the Welsh classes for twenty years, creating the now famous Starlight strain of Welsh mountain pony. Many outstanding descendants are in the United States today, including Liseter Shooting Star, winner of two Grand Champions, one Reserve Grand Champion, 24 Champions, 1 reserve, 34 Firsts, and 5 Seconds for Mrs. Jean du Pont of Newtown Square, Pennsylvania.

As a result of the Welsh pony's comeback in recent years, the vast majority of our stock today comes from ponies imported from England to the United States since 1947. In checking any current pedigree, one persistently comes across the names of three great English breeders.

At Plas Llewelyn, Abergele, North Wales, Miss Margaret Broderick founded the renowned Coed Coch stud in the 1930s. Welsh ponies with

The two types of Welsh presentation today. Above is Liseter Shooting Star, high-scoring Welsh pony for 1963 with Dean Noonkester, handler for Liseter Farm, Newtown Square, Pennsylvania. Below is Imported Coed Coch Bwneath, Grand Champion Welsh Stallion in hand and harness, owned by George B. North of Beaverton, Oregon.

this prefix to their names have since made history and been sent all over the world, especially to the United States. The blood of Coed Coch Madog, Coed Coch Glyndwr, and Coed Coch Meilyr is among the most popular here. When Miss Broderick died in 1962, arrangements were made for this famous stud to continue.

The Criban Stud, founded by Mr. Howell W. Richards of Breconshire, South Wales, likewise produced many outstanding champions. This, the oldest Welsh pony stud in existence, has records dating back for two hundred years during which time its great ponies have been innumerable. Here in the United States the blood of Criban Monarch, Criban Victor, Criban Button, and others is highly prized. Since Mr. Richards' death in 1963, the Criban Stud has been carried on by his son.

The Revel Stud, owned by Mr. Emrys Griffiths, has in recent years gained renown by dominating the Royal Welsh Agricultural Society Show. During the past five years this stud has exhibited only eight ponies, winning five championships and three reserves. Revel Brandy, Revel Gold, Revel Midnight, and several Revel mares have produced superior offspring in this country.

When studying a pedigree, one can identify imported ponies in two ways. They always have an asterisk in front of their name, e.g. *Shalbourne Pendragon, and nearly always two registration numbers will be listed, the American one followed by the English one in parentheses. Any time you find the letter B in front of a Welsh's registration number, it means he is a Section B pony or over 12.2 hands.

Among the people who have done much to bring the Welsh to prominence in this country are Mrs. Joan Mackay-Smith of White Post, Virginia, who has imported and bred many outstanding Welshes and is recognized as one of the foremost authorities and judges of the breed; Mrs. J. Austin du Pont of Newtown Square, Pennsylvania, whose efforts have immensely helped the reorganized Welsh Pony Society of America and whose beautiful Liseter Hall Farm has produced many champions; Mr. and Mrs. George A. Fernley of Plymouth Meeting, Pennsylvania, whose importations in the early 1950s were most valuable; Mrs. Charles Iliff of Arnold, Maryland, whose Severn Oaks Welshes have won in both show and racing competition; Mrs. D. G. Rockwell of King, Ontario, whose Ardmore Stud has brought the Welsh to prominence in Canada; Lithglow Pony Farm of Richmond, Virginia, championing the cause of Section B Welshes; Harold W. Driver of New Market, Virginia, pioneer in the racing Welsh; Mr. and Mrs. A. H. Spitzer of Pleasant Plains, Illinois, Heatherstone Enterprises of Baraboo, Wisconsin, and Clyde A. Richardson of Columbiana, Ohio, all enthusiastic followers of the Welsh as a fine harness pony; Robert H. Hinckley of Eden, Utah, president of the Welsh Pony

A stallion class at the Royal Welsh Show. This is how the English exhibit them.

A pair of matched Welsh ponies under harness display typical loose floating stride. Owner-driver is Mrs. J. Austin du Pont of Newtown Square, Pennsylvania.

Mares and foals from the herd of R. H. Wright, Jr., at Columbus, Georgia.

Society, who has used the Welsh so successfully as surefooted trail ponies.

Most of the Welsh ponies in this country are Section A in height, but the Section B group is becoming more and more popular due to the increasing demand for a larger pony for hunting and jumping. The Welsh pony has the required courage and disposition, and the Section B has the size.

In recent years, in order to produce ponies between thirteen and fourteen hands, the Welsh was frequently crossed with the Arabian, the Thoroughbred, the Chincoteague Island pony, the Saddle Horse, even the Tennessee Walker. The results were most successful, for the Welsh has a high capacity for transmitting his best qualities. Exceptionally good show-type animals are often produced through well-selected crosses to the Welsh, particularly hunters and jumpers.

So many of these ponies became available that the Halfbred and Crossbred Welsh Registry was started for them in 1959 by the Northwest Welsh Pony Club. Its purpose is to record and protect animals with not less than half Welsh parentage and to increase their worth to both seller and buyer. Until the registry was conceived, unscrupulous or misinformed owners of ponies passed off anything larger than a Shetland but smaller than a horse as a Welsh pony. Most had no Welsh blood, many were poor specimens, all of which reflected upon the true Welsh pony. Now a buyer can demand a certificate showing the animal's breeding.

A Halfbred Welsh has one fully registered Welsh parent and an unregistered parent of any breed or combination of breed. A Crossbred Welsh has one fully registered Welsh parent and one fully registered parent of any other breed. There is no height limit. All colors and color combinations are acceptable. The registry operates with the approval and assistance of the Welsh Pony Society of America.

Welsh ponies may be bought directly from breeders or trainers, at production sales or at public auctions like the famous Maryland Pony Breeders Auction at Timonium. A registered yearling can be had for $100 and up, depending upon quality and breeding. A trained, seasoned Welsh will run $300 to $1000. An outstanding breed champion or show pony will run from $1500 up.

Originally the Welsh was presented in the show ring as a "fitted" pony like the Shetland and Hackney—high-stepping in fine harness, whip-handled in model classes to gain the extreme brilliance sought traditionally by Midwest horsemen. But in recent years the vast majority of Welsh followers have come to love the pony for its natural beauty, without the use of artificial aids such as heavy shoes, tail cruppers, side checks, and the like. With its rich flowing mane and its daisy-cutting glide, the Welsh possesses a unique style, they say, and he should be presented naturally in the show ring to bring this forth. They insist he is not meant to be a high-stepping pony, and patterning him after the Shetland and Hackney only leads him down a blind alley already dominated by these breeds.

Perhaps one of the most perceptive observations on the subject has been given by Anne, Duchess of Rutland, in an article in the *Welsh Pony and Cob Society Journal* of 1964. After a visit to the United States, she said:

"The 'fitted' pony with its long weighted hooves and false, or set, tail is something we do not have in this country (England)—and in my opinion the very type we do not want. So many of these ponies seem to have long heads, shallow bodies, peacocky carriage, and very little bone.

"A great deal of this is achieved by the conditions under which the ponies are kept. High protein rations with very little bulk to shrink the stomach and give the light-waisted look. Rubber- or plastic-lined hoods, even in midsummer, to sweat the neck and shoulders, and clipping the forelock and hogging the mane for about eight inches behind the poll to give the effect of a thinner or finer throat. Many ponies wear rattling slave chains around their fetlocks to make them pick their feet up and are 'whip-trained' to make them suspicious and keep their ears pricked and

Golden Glory, Welsh Cob stallion, owned by Samuel K. Martin of Far Hills, New Jersey.

eyes popping watching their handler. Often this results in the pony becoming so nervous that it is necessary to have someone behind carrying a whip when it is led out to show its action. (These people are known as 'trailers' and are prohibited under official American show rules.)

"The outcome of all this training is a neurotic animal that dashes about in a state of hysterical frenzy rather than with the somewhat swashbuckling arrogance which is such a characteristic of the Welsh mountain pony."

In recent years rules for showing the Welsh have been changed to follow the English manner of presenting him naturally. In a model class the overstretched show pose is out; the judge must tell the handler to stand his pony up straight. Yearlings must be shown barefoot, and any older shod pony wearing pads or carrying additional weight of any description shall be disqualified. Also, ponies wearing spoon cruppers, quarter boots, humane tail braces, switches and wigs or any ponies whose tails have been nicked, gingered or put in a tail set for the class entered shall be disqualified. The sections offered by the Welsh Pony Society and American Horse Shows Association are:

Lithglow True Poet, Section B Welsh, glides easily over a three-foot hurdle at National Welsh Show, Devon, Pennsylvania.

1. Welsh Breeding Classes (Model)
2. Welsh Pleasure Pony (English, Western, Trail ponies, Driving, and Combination)
3. Welsh Roadster (Cart and Under Saddle)
4. Welsh Formal Driving Pony
5. Welsh Fine Harness Pony
6. Welsh Hunter and Jumper Pony

In Welsh Formal Driving Classes, the pony is presented in fine harness equipment, but without any artificial appliances. Here is where the true Welsh "shooting action" or daisy cutting shows off best.

Awards are given annually to the pony accruing the most number of winning points in each section. No other pony can claim such a range of competitive activity for children and adults.

"A champion Welsh gains greatness on its own merits, not by superficial showmanship," says one avid follower. "Only in this way will the breed flourish and have its gentle disposition, natural beauty, ability, intelligence, and stamina all recognized. The appeal of the Welsh is not as an animal to be exploited merely as a show ring entertainer, but as a worthy and gentle companion for children and adults who have fallen under the spell of its charm."

And every year more and more people come under the spell of this charm.

Chapter 5

Pony of the Americas

It's hard to believe that any new breed of pony, starting from scratch in 1955, could in a matter of a decade have supporting it a club boasting over twenty-five hundred members from just about every state in the United States, also from Canada, Mexico, Venezuela, Great Britain, and Singapore, a registry of almost five thousand of its kind, a fine monthly magazine, an annual International Show with nearly five hundred entries, a breed promotional sale that grows bigger every year, shows and classes across the country and, above all, serve his original purpose of providing pleasure for thousands of kids. But the Pony of the Americas, or POA as he is better known, has done it.

What does this incredible animal look like?

He's a 46–54-inch pony with Appaloosa coloring, a Western-type using pony for youngsters up to seventeen years of age. By "using" is meant all the classes and competitions and applications that have grown up around the Western stock horse. In size the pony is strong and large enough for a man to break and train, yet small enough for the nearly grown boy or girl to ride and be in proportion with the mount. The ideal type is a happy medium of Quarter horse and Arabian in miniature with Appaloosa coloring.

Home base for this pony is Iowa where Mr. and Mrs. Leslie Boomhower, Mr. and Mrs. Nick Litzel, and Mr. and Mrs. George Barrett, all of Mason City, conceived the idea of forming a new breed after seeing some Appaloosa-colored ponies under fifty-two inches in height. Joining them in forming the club in January 1955 were Robert Wilson, Dr. Fowler B. Poling of Wichita, Kansas, and R. D. Corette of Butte, Montana.

What really whetted the interest of Mr. Boomhower, a lawyer by profession, was the fact that the year before a small Appaloosa mare which he had bred to a Shetland pony produced him a fine Appaloosa colt of pony size which he called Blackhand. The challenge of genetics involving both color and size took hold of the group and all became impassioned with the idea of producing a breed of pony that would be both colorful and useful.

Since there was no real Western-type stock pony for kids in existence and since the Quarter horse was booming like no other modern breed (the Appaloosa horse was not far behind) it was only natural that the pony idea follow a Western-style pattern of development. It would serve a new area of juvenile riding without conflicting with Shetlands, Hackneys, or any other breed.

Most people think of the spotted Appaloosa horse as originating in the Northwest. Actually, there have been polka dot or spotted horses throughout history. But the Nez Perce Indians who inhabited the Palouse country between the Snake, Clearwater, and Palouse Rivers where Oregon, Washington, and Idaho all come together, are credited with having produced the Appaloosa. They took a fancy to spotted mustangs running wild, captured some, and, by careful breeding, isolated a strain of horse that was strong, colorful, and intelligent. By their efforts they became the only American Indians to improve a breed of animal. For their efforts they were driven to ruin.

The tribe, inhabiting prime land wanted by settlers, was restricted to

Blackhand, shown with Danny Boomhower up, is No. 1 in POA registry, a halter and performance champion and outstanding sire. Originally owned by Leslie Boomhower of Mason City, Iowa, he is now the property of Mr. and Mrs. Dee Sayles of Winona, Washington.

a reservation which shrank as more settlers arrived. When the Walla Walla band of the Nez Perce no longer had sufficient grazing land to support its beloved spotted horses, it rebelled. In 1875, under Chief Joseph, some 190 men, with more than 400 women and children, cattle and a horse herd estimated at 3000 head, fought skirmishes with the U. S. Cavalry, followed the nightmarish Lolo trail across Idaho's jagged mountains to Montana, where they thought freedom and grazing land would be theirs. At the now famous Battle of Big Hole the U. S. Army attacked again, and the result was decimation for both sides. The Indians retreated back into the mountains, hoping and struggling to reach Canada where Sitting Bull had found his peace, but fifty miles from the border they were surrounded, defeated, and forced to surrender. Bitterest of all was the confiscation of their spotted horses, which were driven to Fort Keogh on the Yellowstone and sold.

Hadden's Tanka, Champion POA performance pony, takes a three-foot jump with bare-back rider.

Through the years the Appaloosa strain survived, and undoubtedly some of the smaller descendants have contributed in a lasting and important way to the spotted pony in Iowa. But Mexico, Venezuela and other parts of South America had some fine spotted ponies, so when a name was sought for the breed by Mr. Boomhower and his group, they decided upon Pony of the Americas as being most representative. Then it was discovered that England, Scotland, and Germany had long produced them for circus use. As a consequence, importations of what have proven to be foundation sires were made from all of these areas.

Since there was and still is a shortage of stock to produce the POA, cross breeding had to be resorted to. Dark mares, preferably blacks, browns, and bays, are mated to a bright-colored Appaloosa or leopard stallion. If the stallion is oversized, the mare must be small, or vice versa, for the offspring will usually mature between the sizes of the parents. Dark-colored mares tend to produce dark offspring which, if Appaloosa-marked, will generally hold their markings better than light sorrels or palominos.

Though the color genes of Appaloosa are dominant, not always does an offspring have the required markings. If a foal is born solid-colored, it may develop Appaloosa colorings as it matures. If it does not, it can't be registered, but may be used for breeding, particularly if a mare. Favorite cross-bred mares which provide the basic size and conformation for the pony are Arab-Shetland, which gives quality, temperament, and size, and Quarter horse-Shetland, which gives substance, mild temperament, and size. Welshes, Shetlands, Galiceños, and good quality grade ponies have also been used.

At maturity, which is considered to be six years of age, the pony must be between 46 and 54 inches in height. Until 1964 the maximum height was 52 inches, but this was raised to accommodate those people who wanted a shade larger pony for older children to use for cutting, calf roping, trail rides, and hunter classes.

Registration of the POA is done by color. That is, the pony must show one of the six basic Appaloosa markings in order to be eligible. These are spotted blanket, white blanket, leopard, snowflake, frost, and marbling. The white blanket may contain diamond spots (in the shape of a diamond), squaw spots (round or egg-shaped), or teardrop spots (elongated like a tear). Snowflakes are white spots of varying but small sizes scattered over part or all of a dark-colored pony. Frost is scattered white hairs over the body of a dark pony. Marbling appears as varnish marks on a roan body.

No single color or pattern can be called the true POA color, for all are part of the breed. Some colors and patterns are more gaudy than others and as a consequence are more popular, but this is a matter of personal taste. The spotted blanket over the rump with dark forequarters appears most frequently.

Five other physical characteristics help to distinguish the breed. First is white sclera around the eye, giving it a resemblance of the human eye. The white is on the eyeball itself around the colored iris.

Second is the vertically striped hoof, tough and flinty, with a "laminated" look. On some POAs this shows prominently on all four hoofs; others may have it on but one hoof and then it appears only after cleaning and careful inspection.

The third is particolored skin and one of the most telltale signs of the breed. This mottled skin is always evident in the genital region and often appears around the soft skin of the lips, muzzle, nostrils, or eyes.

The fourth is a sparse mane and tail which not all POAs have but they tend toward this characteristic.

The last is varnish marks, most common with roan coloration. Actually these are groupings of predominently dark hairs on a basically light-colored pony. Varnish marks are found on the nose and face, above the eye, on the point of the hip, behind the elbow, and in the gaskin and stifle region. This is often called marbling and is what generally distinguishes an Appaloosa pony from a roan one.

Good POA conformation follows Quarter horse lines. The body is round and well muscled with that solid, chunky look and the sturdy, stock-horse neck, head rather refined along Arab lines, slightly dished and possessing a good-natured alertness.

All POAs are tentatively registered. The letter "T" is placed in front of the registration number until the pony reaches maturity. At that time he is checked over by an authorized inspector of the association or a veterinarian. If height and color specifications are met the "T" is dropped and the pony given permanent registration. The club also stresses that no pony with pinto or albino coloring is eligible for registration though it may have Appaloosa characteristics that would seem to make it acceptable. Nor will any pony whose sire or dam was pinto or albino be accepted. Such blood dilutes and generally spoils Appaloosa coloring.

Get of Sire Class shows three different POA color variations. These youngsters are all by Blackhand No 1.

The famous Dragon No. 103 is shown here cutting figure-8's for his youthful rider. Foaled in Mexico in 1946, he has sired more POA ponies than any other and is also a performance champion.

At this writing, the POA registry is open. Any pony that can qualify will be accepted. By 1970 the books may be partially closed. That is, a pony to be eligible must have at least one parent of POA registration. By so doing, the blood will be concentrated, and some day it is conceivable that the books will be entirely closed to outside blood.

Pony of the Americas Shows are divided into two sections—breed or halter classes, and performance classes.

In halter classes, POAs are shown the same as Shetlands with three exceptions. First, the use of heavy shoes to develop extreme motion or "action" is frowned upon since the club is out to develop a child's Western using pony for comfortable, safe, and practical riding. Second, when the POA is parked or lined up for the Judge's inspection, the pony is never

Norma Jean O'Conner happily rides Stewart's Danny Boy, 1963 National POA Champion and winner of many performance classes. He is owned by John Ludwig of Mohnton, Pennsylvania.

stretched, but is posed in a Hunter's stance, enabling the Judge to see each leg of the pony from both sides clearly and distinctly. Third, the POA is trimmed in Quarter horse style with a roached mane. A clot of hair is also left long over the withers to provide a handhold for the child in mounting, dismounting, and for the purposes of safety when riding bareback. The tail is trimmed and pulled so that the end is even with the top of the hocks.

No tack is permitted in the showing of any stallions, mares, or geldings of any age group. The purpose is to exhibit these animals in as natural a condition as possible. Ponies need not be shod.

Most of the halter class entries are shown by adults, particularly at the more important shows which have championships at stake, but kids reign supreme in the performance classes, and a lot of them there are. Western Pleasure, Western Stock Seat, calf cutting, barrel racing, pole

Kids ride their spotted Indian ponies hard in the 220-yard dash at International POA Show.

bending, stock pony, flat racing, and a host of costume classes mostly Nez Perce Indian style or Cowboy.

An interesting juvenile event is the Trail Class in which ponies proceed through an obstacle course at a walk with a comparatively loose rein. Rider must open and close a gate while mounted. Mount must walk over logs, cross a bridge, pass a boy shooting an air gun, proceed between two logs, stop while rider puts on and takes off a raincoat. The pony proceeds to a trailer where he must load and back out; rider and mount then walk to the finish line. Ponies are judged and penalized on the number of balks and refusals to go through or over obstacles.

POA classes are divided into two height divisions, 46–50 inches and over 50–54 inches. A two-inch difference between the POA top height of 54 inches and the minimum Appaloosa Horse Club height of 56 inches is maintained to distinguish between the two breeds.

The POA is first and foremost a children's working pony, and the kids are the ones who gain the most fun from it. Shows have many novice classes which encourage youngsters to begin riding in the approved Western manner. International awards are given annually to top halter and performance ponies based on a point system. POA show rules have been patterned after those of the American Horse Shows Association, the Appaloosa Horse Club, and the American Quarter Horse Association so that children learn to compete skillfully in the various events which go to make up the performance horse world. These young adults who grow up riding and competing with POAs move on to horses with a sound understanding of horsemanship and, above all, good sportsmanship.

Another important advantage, and a prime reason for the POA's popularity explosion, is the fact that he's an economical pony to own and show. Most are shown unshod, hence costly shoeing bills are eliminated. Expensive silver equipment is of no significance in any POA class, and in the Indian Costume classes kids usually make their own costumes, the rule being that no more than a hundred dollars can be spent for any turnout. POAs keep easily, are rugged and sound in the Western stock horse manner, and can be trained by almost any child with a little parental assistance and encouragement. That the POA has a good-natured, friendly temperament is borne out by the fact that kids ride stallions in many of the performance classes, proving that these ponies are amenable as well as capable and intelligent.

In the relatively short while that POAs have been with us, certain families with the ability to reproduce quality and color have begun to emerge. In recognition of this, the POAC gives a Proven Producer Award to stallions that have become champions at halter and/or performance. Well known among these sires are:

Name	Registered POA Offspring
Dragon No. 103	143
Corette's Scottish Chieftain No. 18	56
Apache Chief No. 4	47
Na-Na-Su'Kin No. 14	32
Blackhand No. 1	31
Stewart's Danny Boy No. 282	25
Siri Chief No. 2	19

All the above, in addition to being foundation stock, carry with them a colorful background. Mr. Boomhower's original POA, Blackhand, proved to be not only a fine individual but also a sire of such high quality that he was deservedly given the honor of being the first name in the POA registry. Siri Chief has as his sire one of the most famous leopard stallions of all time, Arab Toswirah Alkhar. Stewart's Danny Boy and Apache Chief were both National Champions; Corette's Scottish Chieftain has sired more National Champions to date than any other POA, also the consistently highest-selling offspring. Na-Na-Su'Kin (Kootenai Indian for Little Chief) is a Montana resident and one of the few known descendants of Chief Joseph's Appaloosa herd.

Probably the most interesting POA-foundation story belongs to Dragon, a 50-inch stallion coming from Mexico. Mexico has many small Appaloosas, descendants of Mustang stock which in turn traces back to the Spanish Jennet and Barb blood brought to this hemisphere in the sixteenth, seventeenth, and eighteenth centuries by the conquistadors. These tough little horses have survived not only Nature's relentless pressures but also ranchers and Indians, bounty and hide hunters, farmers and dog meat packers.

Dragon was seen by Ellis Dunn in the state of Michoacán, west of Mexico City, trudging down a dirt road and being ridden by a two-hundred-pound Mexican carrying a sack of corn. Though Dragon was "skinny as a snake," Mr. Ellis, a Texan hunting for POA stock, bought him on the spot for twenty-six dollars. Rafael Nieves of McAllen, Texas, pulled the strings which brought the Appaloosa pony through Mexican customs into this country, a more costly detail than the actual purchase of the pony. With Dragon came some other Appaloosa mares exported officially as dogs, while he was listed as a gelding.

Dragon's pedigree is a skimpy one. His sire is listed simply as *Mexican Appaloosa Stud*, dam as *Mexican Appaloosa Mare*, grandparents as *Unknown*. But because he's no cross-bred, rather a pure Appaloosa Mustang, he reproduces over and over the true marks of the breed. With 143 registered sons and daughters already on the books, he is far and away the most color-potent POA sire to date. Though his children may not possess the show quality of some of the other POA blood lines, they are always real Appaloosas, and in the formation of a breed the stallion that can contribute immensely to the basic characteristic of that breed is bound to have a cherished place in its history. In this regard the rugged little pony from the wilds of Mexico will always be remembered.

Each summer the Pony of the Americas Club holds an International Show in Iowa, Oklahoma, Kansas, or elsewhere in the Great Plains area. Youngsters and adults both compete for a heap of prizes and have a heap of fun. In conjunction with the show a trail ride is held. A group of kids, numbering up to fifty, gather at Perry, Oklahoma, with their ponies and ride to wherever the International Show is to be held. This may be one to three hundred miles and take up to a week to complete, but the kids are well supervised and cared for. Dances and barbecues are held en route, city officials greet them, other riding groups join them for a few miles, making it a memorable experience.

An annual Breed Promotion Sale is conducted by the POA Club each fall at Mason City, Iowa. Ponies from many parts of the country are consigned here, and the public has its chance to buy the best of young and old stock. Prices run as high as $1000, $1500, even $2000 or more. One of the top prices at this sale was for Champion Corette's Nez Perce, which brought $2650.

POA champion stallions of proven breeding ability bring amounts of several thousand dollars when they occasionally change hands. In 1963 Blackhand No. 1 was purchased at a dispersal sale for $7750, and other famous POA herd sires have been bought privately from time to time

Randy Rollins of Hollis, Oklahoma, rides his Beaver's Domino in a barrel racing event. This stallion is considered one of the greatest performance ponies of the POA breed.

for $5000 or more. But a good child's pony can be had as a yearling or two-year-old for $200 to $400, and whatever training that is given to the pony, roping or barrel racing or just pleasure riding, will increase its value accordingly.

As so often happens when a new breed becomes exceedingly popular, a second registry springs up. In this case it is the National Appaloosa Pony, Inc., a breed registry for those Appaloosa ponies which because of height limits would not otherwise qualify for registry. With headquarters at Rochester, Indiana, the registry was begun in March 1963 and has had a remarkable growth in a short period, probably because it registers ponies in heights not acceptable to the POA Club. It has two classifications of Appaloosa ponies. Class A is 40 to 48 inches, and Class B is 48 to 56 inches.

The registry already contains well over fifteen hundred ponies of breeders and owners in forty states. More than nine hundred members have joined the National Appaloosa Pony Club, which has full-time inspectors who screen each registration application to make certain the pony meets specifications. Lip tattooing is also recommended by the club and done by the fieldmen as a means of positively identifying ponies even though their coat patterns may change in later life, as often happens.

An annual national show and sale is held each year in Indiana or elsewhere in the Midwest where the organization is particularly strong. The program includes reining, driving, jumping, and racing events, as well as halter and pleasure riding classes.

But no matter what the club or registry, the spotted pony has found a place in the hearts of kids and adults across the country. New though he is, his blood has been around a long time and is instilled in many phases of history in our country and elsewhere in the world. Now that he has another job to do, there is little doubt that he will succeed. He already has.

Chapter 6
The Americana

The latest, all-new addition to the pony world is a high-stepping bundle of charm and grace called the Americana. Created here in this country in 1962 by crossing the Shetland with the Hackney pony, he is intended to be a miniature Saddlebred type of show pony. From the shows in which he has already appeared, he is all this and more.

The idea of the cross is not new. It was tried back in the late 1940s to produce the Harness pony division which declined into the Long-Tailed Hackney class we have today. This time the idea was organized under wiser planning by men of considerable experience, so there seems to be no threat of a return of earlier consequences.

Late in the summer of 1961, Mr. C. C. Bales of Atlanta, Georgia, broached the possibilities of creating the new breed to Asa Hutchinson of Ada, Oklahoma, and Vern Brewer of Gainesville, Texas, as something to consider seriously. The three men were at that time, and still are, breeders of registered Shetlands of the highest quality, with a combined experience of well over fifty years. Meeting a few weeks later, all agreed that the idea had merit if approached correctly.

Their desire was to produce a pony larger in size than the average Shetland and smaller than the Hackney. It had to have good disposition and conformation, and high animated action when conditioned for the show ring. It also had to be suitable for riding and other practical uses when these were desired by children. The goal was an all-purpose pony with beauty and class.

Being breeders and admirers of Shetlands, they considered the Shetland as contributing half of the foundation blood. They believed that the Shetland's disposition, conformation, and size would provide the basis for the type of pony they wanted to develop as a breed. The Hackney would contribute the action, animation, and style. There was considerable discussion as to whether they should permit the Welsh to be used as a cross. Projecting their thinking into the future, they could visualize considerable difference of opinion when the time arrived for breeders to agree on a model of true type for the new breed if more than one cross were permitted. The final decision favored only the Shetland-Hackney mating.

The three men spent considerable time and money sounding out breeders all over the country, asking whether the idea had any merit or appeal to them, and suggestions were welcomed. Most everyone thought the cross would produce a very desirable pony with great show possibilities. Enthusiasm began to grow.

Late in December 1961 it was definitely decided to start the new breed, but two big questions loomed. A suitable name for the breed, and who would own and operate the registry and provide the money to finance the project. The success or failure of the venture swirled around the original three men, so they put up the money and now own the registry, which is located in Winfield, Kansas, with G. L. Booth the recording secretary.

Since the breed originated here in this country, they wanted a name as American as apple pie, hence chose Americana. Notice of the new breed was announced immediately by advertising, and details of the breed program and registration requirements drawn up.

To be eligible for registration, the applicant had to be the result of a cross between a Shetland registered with the American Shetland Pony Club and a Hackney registered with the American Hackney Horse Society and foaled after January 1, 1963. This last eliminated some old-timers who might have come in and been ringers.

Another rule is that an Americana pony produced from a Hackney-Shetland mating may be crossed back to a Shetland to further reduce the size if desired. Colorwise, the Americana has all the variations of the Shetland, including silver dapples, golden dapples, palominos, and pintos, but dark colors like bays, browns, and blacks will most likely prevail because Hackneys are always dark-colored and theirs is strong blood.

Maximum height at maturity was set at 46 inches, and here again considerable thought was given to the necessity of avoiding the harness pony pitfalls a few years earlier. (See the Hackney chapter.) By far the most prominent suggestion prior to setting the rules was that the height limit be an inch or two more. Most everyone would have preferred a larger pony, but from past experience most were convinced it could very well mean suicide to the breed in a short while.

The Americana Club sponsors and sanctions classes in which entries are restricted to registered Americana ponies not exceeding 46 inches in height. It was felt at the time the group was organized that the Americana pony produced from a good quality sire and dam would be second to no other breed in conformation and beauty. The relatively few foal

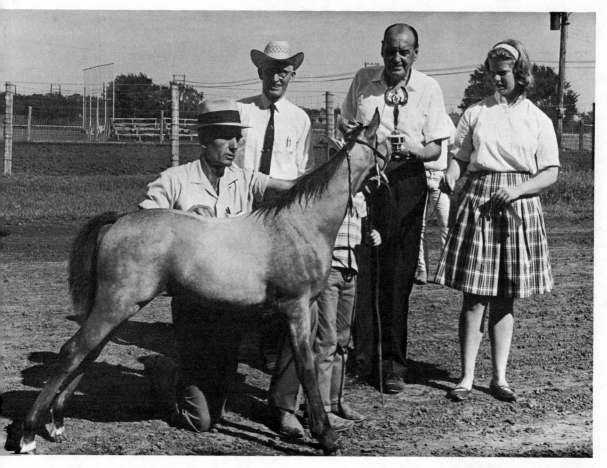

Grand Ace, a young Americana stud colt, sniffs his winning trophy at Americana Show in Winfield, Kansas.

crops produced so far bear this out. Only the Hackney might be expected to exceed them in action, and the number of these under 46 inches with a show foot is negligible.

After a sufficient number of Americanas have been registered, the basic Shetland-Hackney cross will be eliminated and only offspring from two registered Americanas will be eligible for registration. In any cross-breeding program designed to produce a new breed or type, there is always the genetic problem of throwbacks to one side or the other of the two original families, but the selectivity demanded by show ring competition and a tight standard should eliminate this. All our modern breeds of light horses and ponies were begun as crosses or strengthened in recent years by outside blood. Then by means of rigid selectivity they were quite quickly solidified into the conformation and type desired.

Americana rules permit the cross to be made either way, Hackney stallion to Shetland mare or vice versa. Nine times out of ten a small, high-quality Hackney stallion is used on a band of well-chosen Shetland mares, for two reasons. Most of the Americana breeders are Shetland breeders, and then Hackneys being expensive, it's cheaper to buy a stallion than a band of mares.

To date, more than a thousand Americanas have been registered, and the club boasts over two hundred and fifty members from forty states and Canada. The club has ten districts, the directors of which form the Board of Governors, the so-called guiding light of the club. The annual dues of five dollars go into a special fund for promoting the breed.

The Americana Jubilee, held each October, combines the annual convention, National Finals Show, and a breed promotion sale. Only top-quality Americanas appear at this, the major show for the breed, for they must have placed in a district show in order to enter. Thus the poorer stock is sorted out early in the game.

Like the other pony breeds, the Americana has two show divisions— halter or "hand" and performance. Ponies in the hand classes are judged 60 percent on conformation and 40 percent on action. Weanlings (six months to a year) must not be shod, nor shall any artificial device such as lead (inside the hoof), chains, etc., be used. Shoeing of yearlings is optional. A yearling must not exceed 43½ inches in height at the withers, two-year-olds must not exceed 45 inches, and three-year-olds and up must not exceed 46 inches.

In the hand classes, the Americana is shown in a stretched position, like the Shetland and Hackney. At the National Finals, a Grand Champion stallion and mare, also Reserve of each, are chosen from the winners of the individual classes.

The performance division to date includes fine harness and roadster classes as well as children's riding classes. The fine harness Americana ponies are shown with the same equipment as the American Saddlebred horses wear in their fine harness turnout. This includes overcheck bridles, martingales, and quarter boots. This is entirely different equipment from what other harness ponies wear and distinguishes the Americana as a miniature American Saddlebred.

The National Breed Promotion Sales have been whopping successes so far. The first one, held in 1964, averaged $290 per head for yearlings and weanlings. The top five ponies averaged $825; the top fifteen averaged $532. Top pony of the sale was National Champion Grand Belle, a weanling filly which brought $1200. The National Grand Champion mare, Richardson's Linda, brought $1150. Top stallion of the sale, Bill-Mar's King of Hearts, went for $700. When one considers that these ponies had had very little training other than halter, leading, and stretching, these are good prices for a brand-new breed.

Enthusiasm has run high from the beginning, especially among those who knew the merits of each breed. To them the idea of blending the good-natured, snappy show Shetland with the high-stepping, fiery Hackney and possibly coming up with the classic show pony of all time was so intriguing that few could resist playing the game. To date they have succeeded, for the good Americana is a superb little animal, possessing a finely-chiseled head, bold eye, small spike ears, a body that combines substance with quality. The Hackney spirit shows in his alertness, the Shetland's good nature in his gentleness.

The breed has a long way to go before it is stabilized, but a host of sincere and dedicated people have put considerable time, thought, and effort into this zesty new pony. With a sound organization behind him, with classes for adults and children in using him in shows across the country, the Americana seems destined to achieve its motto: "Today . . . the world's most beautiful foals. Tomorrow . . . the world's most beautiful ponies." Good luck to him.

The Americana, our newest official breed, is a cross between Hackney and Shetland. Refined young mare, Grand Arlene, wins a championship for Vern Brewer of Gainesville, Texas.

Chapter 7

The Connemara

Tight along the Irish seacoast in County Galway lies a wild mixture of rock and crag, peat bogs and heather, small pastures and tilled plots boxed in by stone walls. The region, known as Connemara, still possesses the customs and language of ancient Ireland as well as one of the finest ponies we have today.

Ruggedness of living and stress of storm have enforced the survival-of-the-fittest law upon the Connemara pony and in the process made it one of the sturdiest and soundest in all of horsedom. Connemara ponies have almost never been housed, but lie out in all kinds of weather with no shelter other than rocks and caves. In their youth they run wild up and down the rugged mountains, over the jagged rocks and narrow ledges like mountain goats, a training which makes them eminently suited for hunting and jumping, especially as children's mounts.

A roundup takes place every year generally just before the big Connemara Pony Show at Clifden. Local cowboys catch the ponies by driving them into the low country of bogs and quagmire. As one becomes helplessly stuck, a rope is slipped over his head and he is made captive. Paradoxically the Connemara which has been running free and wild can usually be gentled in a matter of a few days. Stories tell of farmers capturing a pony one day and bicycling down the road to show it the next day, the pony trotting along behind on no more than a lead line.

Horsemen say these are the easiest animals to train and break they have ever come across. Furthermore, they retain what they learn, seldom have to be trained over and over.

The fame of the Connemara as a jumper has spread across the world. Size for size, no member of the equine world can "outlepp him," as the Irish say. In fact, it's been the other way around. Though officially he stands 13 to 14.2 hands and grows to 15 when crossed, he has outjumped 16- and 17-hand horses at some of the greatest events in Europe and the United States.

Colonel Hume Dudgeon's Korbous brought fame to the breed in the

1950s when he won the Irish Three Day Event in the Horse Trials at Harewood against the best Thoroughbred Hunters in the country. His sire was of Arab-Barb blood, his dam a Connemara mare.

Certainly one of the most amazing diminutive jumpers in American history was the Irish-bred, straight Connemara Little Squire. Only 13.2 hands, this remarkable little fellow cleared seven-foot fences, won a peck of ribbons with 160 pounds of rider plus equipment on his back, and in 1939 beat the finest jumpers in the country to win the Open Championship in Madison Square Garden. Said his owner, Danny Shea, "He could jump any kind of a fence that any of the top horses could jump. He didn't care if it were the widest or the highest, his heart was up to it, and he would try anything he was asked."

Another fantastic Connemara jumper was The Nugget. Stanislaus Lynch, well-known Irish equestrian competitor and authority, describes him as follows: "Probably one of the greatest performers in show jumping history was an over-grown Connemara named The Nugget. This animal was only about fifteen hands high, but at the International Horse Show at Olympis, London, in 1935 he cleared seven feet two inches! He won over three hundred first prizes, one hundred cups, and innumerable other prizes. In the years when prize money was comparatively insignificant by present-day standards he earned over £4500 (or close to $25,000) in prize money!"

The most brilliant show jumper in Ireland today, possibly in the world, is a Connemara bay gelding called Dundrum. This courageous but docile-dispositioned fifteen-hand animal was sired by Little Heaven from a mare out of the Connemara hills. He first pulled a grocer's cart along the village streets of Dundrum. Proving too impetuous for this, he ended up in the hands of horse trainer-trader James Wade, Sr., who couldn't sell him. His son, Tommy, took him over and made history, Dundrum becoming champion of the Royal Dublin Show for four years against Europe's finest jumpers.

In 1959 at Wembley he jumped 7' 2" and won that championship in 1961. But 1963 was Dundrum's greatest year. In July, with Tommy Wade, his youthful owner-rider, he won the celebrated King George V trophy, presented by Queen Elizabeth. This is the same trophy won by the famous American jumper Nautical. Dundrum's greatest triumph came a month later in August when he won the Aga Khan trophy against the finest international jumpers and riders. For fourteen years no Irish jumper had won this huge gold trophy, emblematic of King of the World's Jumping Horses, until the little bay from Connemara came along and "lepped" his heart out.

These stories are told early in this review of the Connemara not to belabor a point but to show the indomitable character and strength of this

Connemara ponies rail birding at Hideaway Farm, Geneseo, New York.

pony from the west hills of Ireland. Certainly the fact that they spend their early days roving over rough country, bouncing over walls, balancing on ledges of rock, avoiding boggy quagmires, gives them a super sense of balance and timing, sharpens their intelligence, and inculcates an instinctive ability to get out of trouble. All these traits are priceless for show jumping or cross-country work such as fox-hunting and point-to-point racing.

Physically, what do they possess that makes them such super jumpers?

First, they tend to have tremendous propelling power in their hindquarters. Real good bone and muscle is what jets them over the huge barriers. They are powerful in a practical way rather than refined.

Second, they have good big sloping shoulders which give them the initial spring and cushions their landing. Despite all the jumping they do, Connemaras are amazingly sound animals.

Winner of Intermediate Division of U. S. Three-Day Combined Training Event at Woodstock, Vermont, is An Tostal, eight-year-old Connemara stallion owned and ridden by Mrs. Bruce Read of East Pepperell, Massachusetts.

How did these rugged fellows come about?

The history of the Connemara is woven in legend as is so much of Ireland's past. Most likely, before the importation of any foreign blood, a breed of hardy native ponies existed on the west coast of Ireland. These may have come from Norsemen or from Wales. Legend has it that when the Spanish Armada was wrecked off the coast of Ireland, in 1588, Andalusian horses swam ashore and subsequently crossed with the local blood. More likely the Spanish Barbs and Jennets which went to the New World with de Soto and Cortés also reached west Ireland in the sixteenth and seventeenth centuries through the then thriving seaport of Galway, which traded heavily with Spain and is still the gateway to Connemara. At various times up to the middle of the nineteenth century Arabian blood was infused into the Connemara, and characteristics of these strains are evident today.

From 1850 to 1900 considerable outcrossing to other breeds was done indiscriminately. One of the more successful ones was to Welsh Cob stallions, carried on about 1890 by both district boards and private owners. Descended from this line was Cannon Ball, one of the foundation sires in the Connemara Registry. Another famous early sire, Powder, by Prince Llwewllyn who was a Welsh Cob, figures prominently in many of the best old mares in the Masm Cross district.

The government injudiciously crossed in Thoroughbred, Halfbred, and Hackney blood, but much of it passed out of the picture because the foals were not hardy enough to survive the stringent weather conditions and lack of shelter.

Professer J. C. Ewart of Edinburgh University made a study of the Connemara pony in 1900, pointing out that these ponies, when bred to horses all over Ireland had "enhanced their reputations for vigor, hardiness, and intelligence." He praised the breed as having great possibilities but warned that unless systematic breeding could be established, the breed would become extinct.

In 1923 the Connemara Pony Breeders Society was founded to improve the breed from within, not by further outcrossing. A hundred mares of the best stock were obtained, along with free service privileges to a carefully selected group of top stallions. The most promising ten to twelve yearlings were chosen and turned loose on the heath to graze and subsist without shelter or extra fodder. After two and a half years the final selection was made from those that survived. Thus was the Connemara pony brought back.

Though an occasional Connemara pony came to America before World War II, it was not until 1951 that the first importation for breeding purposes was made. Two stallions, Lavalley Pride and Tully Nigger, along with four mares were brought over by the late George L. Ohrstrom for his Whitewood Stud, The Plains, Virginia. These ponies were used by his grandchildren for fox-hunting in the beautiful hunt country around Middleburg and as a nucleus of a herd in this country.

Shortly thereafter Mrs. Magruder Dent of Greenwich, Connecticut, imported a small herd of Connemaras that were the foundation stock for her grandchildren's hunting ponies. The herd is now owned by Mr. and Mrs. Magruder Dent, Jr., of Polaris Farm, Charlottesville, Virginia, who have imported other Connemaras, including the well-known Farravine Boy, sire of champion ponies in England and Ireland.

In the early 1950s the late Frank Murchison imported a large group of Connemaras to his cattle ranch near San Antonio, Texas. When he died, the herd was sold to William B. Dolph of Ivy, Virginia. Head sire of this herd is Champion Texas Hope, producer of some of the finest show-quality Connemaras in this country.

Two Connemara ponies and a Thoroughbred hunter form the mounts for the Magruder Dent family of Charlottesville, Virginia.

The children of Mr. and Mrs. Edward Harris of Geneseo, New York, all mounted on Connemara Ponies.

Mrs. Bruce Read of East Pepperell, Massachusetts, imported a band of five mares for breeding. Her Connemaras have won in point-to-points, competing against horses, and at Hunter Trials, Horse Shows, and the New England Regional Rally. She is secretary of the American Connemara Society.

Mrs. Charles Case of Avon, New York, imported the well-known stallion, Tooreen Laddie, now owned by Mrs. Edward C. Harris, Jr., of Geneseo, New York. Laddie has been used extensively at stud in the New England area and produced some outstanding winners.

In the Midwest, Le Wa Farm of Lake Forest, Illinois, assembled a large herd of Connemaras and has sent stock to Washington, Oregon, Missouri, and other parts of the country.

The biggest herd of Connemaras in the United States belongs to Mr. and Mrs. Robert H. Wright, Jr., of Columbus, Georgia. Nine mares and a stallion comprised the first importation; the second consisted of forty-three head, the largest shipment of Connemaras ever to come to the United States. These ponies were selected by Stanislaus Lynch and included several champions at Dublin, Clifden, and other Irish shows.

Thus the Connemara began to mushroom across the country. A short five years after the first importation, the American Connemara Pony Society was founded in December 1956 and an American registry was begun. Interest has steadily increased since that time, so that today the Society boasts some two hundred owners and breeders of Connemara Ponies in twenty-seven states, Canada, and Mexico.

The points of the Connemara are as follows:

> Height: 13 to 14.2 hands.
> Color: Gray, black, bay, brown, dun, cream, with occasional roans and chestnuts. Piebalds and skewbalds are not acceptable for registration.
> Type: Body compact, deep, standing on short legs and covering a lot of ground.
> Shoulders: Riding.
> Head: Well-balanced neck and head.
> Characteristics: Clean, hard, flat, measuring approximately seven to eight inches below the knee.
> Bone: Hardiness of constitution, staying power, docility, intelligence, and soundness.

Standards for showing the Connemara, as explained in the American Connemara Pony Stud Book Regulations, are as follows:

A. All Ponies must be shown as typical hunting ponies. Braiding is optional. No ponies may be shown with excessively long toes. No artificial devices may be used. Ponies shall not stand in stretched position.
B. If a division or class states that it is for purebred ponies only, no pony registered in the halfbred division of the Stud Book may enter these classes.
C. For purposes of showing, no pony over two years of age may be shown at an authorized Connemara pony show unless he holds a permanent certificate.
D. For horse show purposes, the rules of the American Connemara Pony Society will coincide with those of the American Horse Shows Association with the following exceptions:
   1. In classes restricted to Connemaras, adults may show ponies unless the class states specifically otherwise.
   2. Stallions may be shown in performance classes.

The American Connemara Pony Stud Book also operates a supplementary registry for Halfbred Connemara ponies, those which have one pure Connemara parent. Many fine hunting ponies and junior jumpers have been obtained by crossing to Connemaras. The interesting part of the Connemara Halfbred regulations is Article 3 which states:

"In the fifth generation, the progeny of a Halfbred Connemara mare or stallion will be eligible for entry in the Purebred Stud Book, provided that, according to the records, all intervening crosses have been to Purebred Connemara ponies only."

This is one of the most sensible rules ever written. It gives a serious breeder some flexibility and allows room for the great individual which occasionally results from an outcross, while still keeping the breed substantially pure. In other breeds, when such outcrossing takes place, it is, perforce, unrecorded.

In their importations of Connemara ponies, and consequently in their breeding programs, Americans have sought hardiness, manners, and good looks. Whether by design or coincidence, most all of the ponies in the United States trace back to Rebel (7) in Volume I of the Irish Stud Book. His descendants—Innishgoill Laddie, Calla Rebel, Lavalley Rebel, Gil, Tiger Gil, Cill Ciarain, Carna Bobby, Tooreen Laddie, Strongbow, Camlin Cirrus—are the basis of American Connemara pedigrees.

Two other important foundation sires are Black Paddy (8) and Connemara Boy (9) in the Irish Stud Book. The latter's blood is carried down

Crepe Suzette, Connemara mare, winner of many pony jumping events, takes a gate over outside course at Deep Run Hunt Club Show in Virginia, Miss Susie Dent up.

by Heather Bell, Derry Boy, Dun Heath, Lavalley Con, Dun Lorenzo, Dun Orphan, and MacDara. The former sired Noble Star, who in turn sired Lavalley Star, Cashel Star, and Clough Droighnean.

Three additional old stallions, Tully Lad, Creganna Winter, and Carna Dun, exerted great influence on the breed, and their blood is carried by many American Connemara ponies.

Certainly, few pony breeds have made the progress here in the short time that the Connemara has. It can only be accounted for by the fact that the pony lives up to all its claims—"capable of carrying an adult in the hunt field, yet gentle and tractable enough for a young child, fearless as a show jumper, yet suitable and steady as a driving pony." From the broad base of popularity that it has established here in less than a decade, the Connemara is sure to grow and enjoy a far-reaching popularity in the years ahead. As the Irishman said, "And sure it couldn't happen ta better horse flesh."

Chapter 8

The Galiceño

One of the most colorful and certainly most practical little horses to come to this country in recent years is the Galiceño (pronounced Gali-SEHN-yo). The "little" part must be emphasized because, though this sturdy fellow from Mexico stands from 12 to 13.2 hands in height, he is not referred to as a pony but as a horse, which in reality he is—in looks, character, and gaits. But he is included here because he falls into the pony height category.

Analyzing the name Galiceño leads one to believe that these horses came originally from the ancient province of Galicia in northwestern Spain. The breed most probably existed there before Columbus discovered America, for the Spanish possessed one of the highest stock-raising cultures in the world during the fourteenth, fifteenth, and sixteenth centuries. This was continued in the New World on the islands of Hispaniola and particularly Cuba which acted as a supply base for Cortés when he invaded Mexico in 1519. Records show that Cortés carried with him sixteen horses of the Spanish jennet type, none of which survived very long but managed to overawe the Indians.

More stock was soon brought to Mexico from Cuba, providing mounts for the conquistadors and allowing the Spanish to extend their control over this area of the world. When Francisco Coronado started his expedition northward to Arizona and New Mexico in 1541, he left Mexico City with a force estimated at 1500 people, 1000 horses, 500 cattle, and 5000 sheep. To put together this number of horses in twenty-two years in what had been a horseless continent required a considerable amount of breeding somewhere. Much of it could have been done in Cuba, but some must have taken place in Mexico itself.

These Spanish jennets were tough and sturdy little animals, well known in Europe for their attractiveness, agility, and ability to carry grown men under light armor. Of course, the Spanish were of small stature in those days and their armor was, for good reason, not the all-protective kind of the English and French knights of chivalry. The Spanish had chivalrously sent heavy-armored knights mounted on ponderous war horses against the invading Moors, who, using no armor at all and riding fast, quick-maneuvering Barb horses from the deserts of North Africa, decimated them.

A change in tactics became necessary, so the Spanish developed a special breed of light horse by crossing the Moorish Barb with local mountain stock and fashioned a light armor consisting mainly of a breastplate. The conquistador on his small prancing jennet became a highly effective and highly respected warrior. It was this combination as much as anything else which established the might of Spain so quickly in the New World.

The Galiceño appears to be the remnant of the old Spanish jennet. He is a pretty little horse, bright and alert, quick to learn—all traits that the jennet had inherited from his Barb ancestry, a breed very similar to the Arabian.

Legend also has it that the conquistadors used the Galiceño to work the silver mines in the mountainous Yucatán district of Mexico. After the silver had been drained dry, the conquistadors turned their Galiceños loose in the mountains where eventually the natives caught some and used them for menial tasks.

In any event the Galiceño remained isolated in the coastal regions of Mexico while thousands of other horses moved northward with the Spanish across the Rio Grande to run wild and form the famous mustang herds after Indian uprisings had set them free to roam the plains. Through the centuries the Galiceño became a forgotten breed. In his isolation he remained relatively pure and highly prized by the natives for his riding ease, courage, endurance, his ability to pull carts and pack supplies. A rare few found their way to the United States but none was ever bred here.

In 1958 the late Harvey Mecom of Liberty, Texas, vacationing in the Yucatán peninsula of Mexico, saw some of the little horses and immediately fell in love with them. He and his wife decided to have a herd back home and began exporting them from the area in large numbers back to their ranch.

Almost at the same time, two other Texans, Glen Bracken of Tyler and C. M. Dolan of Eagle Pass, made a trip to Mexico in search of a new breed that would satisfy the increasing demand for a gentle pleasure riding and contest horse for children and would double as a working horse for adults. When they came across the Galiceño, they knew they had it. They too imported a herd of the sturdy, spirited little fellows, and in December 1959 they organized the Galiceño Horse Breeders Association which today boasts over two hundred members from twenty-seven states and over a thousand purebred Galiceños in the registry started at the same time.

Galiceños have competed successfully in Western classes at various shows across the country. In three areas the breed is particularly strong—Texas, Michigan, and Washington. The Southwestern Exposition and Fat Stock Show at Fort Worth has a most popular Galiceño division of classes as do the Houston and San Antonio shows. In Michigan many Galiceños have competed in halter and performance classes at shows throughout the state.

In the Spokane, Washington, area all the major horse shows since 1961 have included Galiceño classes consisting of Western Pleasure, Spanish Fiesta, and halter events. They have competed and won in open Western and English classes, Saddle Pony, and Pony Jumping as well as at Gymkhanas. In several trail rides, some over a hundred miles long, Galiceños have been right up front with the regular-sized horses.

In February 1964 the Washington Galiceño Horse Club, the first of its kind in the United States, was formed. Two youthful members and their mounts, Miss Calie Snoddy with El Count and Miss Robin Corte with Rose Anita, won Grand Champion and Reserve respectively in the first National

Galiceños are patient horses, as proven here by Vickita who willingly takes the four grandchildren of Mr. and Mrs. Henry Walter of Moses Lake, Washington, for a ride.

Ready for a Galiceño Spanish Costume Class is Dale F. Brannon and his K.W.'s Blackie.

Pony Trail Ride, a timed event. Dale Brannon, a senior club member, was awarded "Man of the Year" in the state of Washington for his work with youth both in the club and in the community.

Club President Walter Johnson was the first importer of Galiceños to the Pacific Northwest. Becoming enthusiastic about the breed, he went to the Gulf of Mexico in February 1960 and brought back three mares and a stallion. They created such a stir and he was so pleased with them that he had others trucked in the following summers. Now there are more than two hundred Galiceños and some thirty breeders in Washington and Idaho.

"The past three seasons," Mr. Johnson says, "I have used Galiceños for big game hunting and packing trips into our steep rugged mountainous country. They perform their work of packing gear and game extremely well, being very sure-footed and cautious. I weigh over two hundred pounds, but my hunting mare, Belita, packs me with ease in the mountains."

Certainly the Galiceño is a breed that catches a horseman's eye and holds his attention. Slim and trim, beautiful in looks and action, they are not designated ponies because they have the action of a full-sized horse, also saddle gaits not seen in a true pony. Actually, they have four gaits—walk, full trot, running walk, and canter. Their running walk is similar to that of the Tennessee Walking horse.

It is interesting to compare this horse of Spanish descent with the Paso Fino of Puerto Rico. Also possessing a running walk, the Paso Fino is descended from the original stock of the Spanish horse ranches estab-

Terry Ovnicek and his 51-inch Galiceño, Maria, win a Western Pleasure class in Washington.

Linda Houghton on Ricardo, 50-inch Galiceño gelding, runs the barrels at Aragone Show in Washington.

lished there in the sixteenth and seventeenth centuries. Other blood—Morgan, Saddle Horse, and Arabian—has heightened this most attractive animal, otherwise he might be the same size as the Galiceño, who would appear to be his cousin.

The Galiceño Horse Breeders Association says its breed was produced by the forces of evolution and not by the hand of man, thus a type distinguishable by many traits was established. He shows good substance, lots of style and rhythm in motion. His natural running walk sets him apart from the pony family. He ranges from 12 to 13.2 hands with the majority falling in the 50- to 52-inch height group, weighs from 625 to 700 pounds, and comes in all solid colors—bay, black, brown, chestnut, sorrel, dun, gray, roan, and a few palominos. No albinos, pintos, or crossbreds are eligible for registration.

The Galiceño head shows character and intelligence by the good width between the eyes and the medium-sized ears, which are smaller in stallions. The body is well muscled, the back short and extremely straight, croup sloping to a moderately high-set tail. Shoulders, thighs, and legs are well muscled and strong; this is how they take the weight they do. The horse is quick and extremely handy on his feet. His natural running walk covers a lot of ground, and this is what makes him such an easy ride, even for long periods of time.

According to show rules, the horse must be shown Quarter Horse style. Western equipment must be used. In halter classes, entries are to be shown in a Western or hunter's pose, not stretched. Only light Western-type shoes can be used, and only a regular Western bit or snaffle with leather chinstrap is permissible.

The Galiceño has come a long way in a short time. That he is a lot of animal he has proven wherever he's been given a chance. His friendly, gentle disposition makes him ideal for the child and the young adult who wants something more horsy than a pony. He is strong enough also to carry the light, even the average adult, if a small nimble mount is desired. Thus the future seems bright for this stalwart from Mexico, who, nearly five hundred years ago, was possibly the first horse to return to the Western Hemisphere.

Chapter 9

Island Ponies

Scattered at various points along the eastern seacoast from Nova Scotia to Florida are isolated herds of wild ponies. The actual histories of these ponies are not known, but the legends that have grown up around them are colorful and possibly true. Wild ponies live on Ocracoke Island in North Carolina and on Sea Island in Georgia, but for this discussion we will stick to those on Chincoteague Island, which are world famous, and those on Sable Island which are probably least known.

Chincoteague Island Ponies of Virginia

The Chincoteague pony got his name from the island of that name located along the coastline of northern Virginia and inhabited mainly by fishermen and chicken growers. It is protected against the buffeting Atlantic tides, storms, and winds by an outer island called Assateague, a long bleak shoal of land, and here is where the wild ponies live as strange remnants of another era.

The ancestors of these ponies, according to one belief, came from a Spanish ship loaded with horses which was wrecked over three hundred years ago on the outer island of Assateague. They broke free of the wreckage and swam ashore where they have remained ever since. Another theory has it that the Chincoteague descends from Indian stock. These swift, light horses, which were of pony size and which the Virginia colonists developed into the quarter-mile-running-horse, an ancestor of today's Quarter horse, originally came from Spanish settlements along the coast of Florida and Georgia. Another way-out story says that these Chincoteague ponies are the only surviving descendants of *Eohippus* that made the grade through prehistoric times, the Ice Age, et al. There's absolutely nothing to support this claim. Either of the first two theories is plausible, with the second being most probable. The ponies most likely sought out this remote refuge as a desperate means of escaping the advance of civilization, or might well have been placed there for breeding purposes by a farmer who died—unromantic though this may be. The only reason they survive today is that no humans have had a desire to take over the land.

Assateague is no lullaby island. In summer it becomes hot and sand flies are so bad that the ponies often wade into the water until only their noses, eyes, and ears are left exposed. In fall and winter the storms are unmerciful, sometimes of hurricane proportions. Spring is the best season for the ponies, but in July comes the annual roundup which takes away most of the young stock, so they fight a difficult battle all year round.

Originally the Chincoteague was a solid-colored pony on the dark side —bay, brown, black, chestnut. Then in order to pep up the pony color-wise, some Western pintos were put into the herd, which didn't help genetically at all. Later Shetland and Welsh stock was crossed in, and the size which had been around 14 hands, diminished to 12 to 13.2 hands as seen today. The colors are mixed now, ranging from pinto to gray, sorrel, bay, and black. No beauty contest winner, the Chincoteague never-theless is a hardy pony with a wonderfully gentle disposition once he's tamed and broken. This makes him ideal for children to learn on and all youngsters to ride. When he is crossed with registered stock such as a small Thoroughbred or Welsh or Arabian, excellent ponies often result. His native endurance and wisdom seem to predominate.

The pony is best known because of the annual roundup called Pony Penning Day, conducted by the Chincoteague Volunteer Fire Department to raise funds for equipment. Members boat their own mounts to Assa-teague Island, round up the wild ponies, drive them to the water. The ponies then swim through a channel of boats to Chincoteague where they run down the main street of town to a big corral. There they are "penned" and the next day the foals sold off at public auction for prices ranging from $50 on up to $250 per head. None of these ponies is regis-tered, but many a happy child from all over the eastern seaboard has come home with a good one.

Pony Penning Day takes place on the last Thursday in July. People come from many states to see the event, and local residents open up their homes for overnight guests because the two small hotels on the is-land can't handle the crowds. If you ever visit Pony Penning Day, be sure to get there a day in advance of the sale and see the roundup of the herd and the swim from the outer to the inner island. Children find the whole event fascinating, from the drive to the corralling to fried chicken dinners and the Ferris wheel.

One word of caution. If you buy a foal, be sure to take extra special care of the little one immediately. At this time of year foals are not yet weaned from their mothers, so the sale amounts to weaning them. Unless the youngster is well attended he may not survive. You will probably have to coax him to eat his first oats or ground feed, even wet his lips a little so he learns to drink. Also, he should be well wormed and given a stock dip to destroy all body and skin parasites.

If you make the trip to Chincoteague, your children will want to stop and see the famous Misty who lives in a nice box stall at the Beebe Ranch owned by George Beebe. Heroine of several books and star of a Disney film, she lives a life of ease now with her offspring. If you also like seafood, especially oysters, don't miss these either. The island is equally famous for them.

The Wild Ponies of Sable Island

The ponies of Sable Island also have a wrecked-ship legend of origin, and in this case it's undoubtedly true. Their home is a glorified sandbar in the Atlantic Ocean about one hundred miles east of Nova Scotia. The island, about twenty miles long and from half to a mile wide, is known to seafarers as "the graveyard of the Atlantic" because of more than two hundred recorded wrecks there. Not a tree is on the island, but ponds and springs provide fresh water.

An estimated two hundred and fifty ponies run wild in herds of from five to fifteen. They graze on beach grass, clover, and wild peavine.

The Sable Island ponies are handsome animals, 13 to 14.2 hands, and often possess exceptionally beautiful manes and tails. Their colors are mostly dark, varying from black, brown, and bay to an occasional palomino, but no pintos. The sandy soil of the island keeps their hoofs worn down and in good shape. As winter approaches, their coats grow long and shaggy for protection against the severe winds and storms which come howling off the Atlantic.

Interestingly, when winter comes, the herds join up and travel together, providing better warmth and protection. The scarcity of winter forage continually takes the lives of the weaker ponies, but in summer when the grass grows green and high, they become sleek and fat. The mares foal from early spring until late in September.

Through the years a few have been broken to ride by the local inhabitants who themselves number only eleven persons, mostly lighthouse attendants and radio operators.

A few years ago these ponies narrowly missed being sold when the Dominion Government called for Tenders (public bids) for their sale and removal from the island. So many people protested that the Prime Minister himself rescinded the order. Thus they live on in their windswept surroundings, lonely fugitives from the past.

Chapter 10
Gaited and Walking Ponies

Two of the most graceful and elegant breeds of ponies that we have today are the Gaited pony properly known as the American Saddlebred pony, and the Walking pony whose correct name is Tennessee Walking pony. Both are discussed in this one chapter because they are closely related in origin and are presented under similar tack, conditions, and dress in the show ring.

The Gaited Pony

The American Saddlebred pony is the height of commanding carriage and graceful movement. From the crisp precision with which he lifts his feet to the spirited toss of his head, he makes it known that he's a monarch in the show pony world. His performance, done always with precision and animation, with gaits of different speeds and rhythms, is a glorious spectacle that you don't soon forget.

The origin of these beautifully groomed, beautifully trained ponies is an interesting one, and for the moment we will have to talk horses to explain it. Back in the 1840s Kentuck Saddlers were a popular riding and driving horse. They lined the hitching posts of every small town square, carried carriages elegantly to church in the Midwest before and particularly after the Civil War. The blood of *Denmark, *Messenger, *Bellfounder, *Copperbottom, all famous colonial stallions (the asterisk before a horse's name always indicates that he was imported), ran strongly in their veins. In the 1870s and 1880s a Saddler became something special, the perfectly-gaited horse for the gentleman to ride and the lady to drive.

Thus came about the various show classes which we have today—the three-gaited, the five-gaited, and fine harness. In the first class he wears a clipped or roached mane and tail; in the last two he carries a full mane and tail.

The three-gaited Saddler is often called a "Walk-Trot" horse and is noted for extreme collection in performing his three gaits, walk, trot, and canter.

Miss Julianne Schmutz winning the World's Championship Five-Gaited Pony title at Kentucky State Fair in 1964 with her brilliant show pony, The American Model. This pair was also Reserve Champion at Lexington and Champion at Illinois State Fair, Oldham County and Miami Charity Horse Show, all in 1964.

"Collection" refers to the horse's impulse to go forward and the rider's restraint on the bit to hold him back. This arches his neck, brings his legs under him, moves his center of gravity farther back so the horse moves with a fiery, near-prancing elegance.

The five-gaited horse is noted for his extreme speed and action, being able to perform the walk, trot, canter, slow gait, and rack. The slow gait is a highly animated stepping movement, the rack a four-beat gait done at near-racing speed or as fast as the horse can travel without losing form. These two gaits are man-taught, though some horses have more ability to learn and perform them than others.

How did the Saddlebred pony come into being?

Within every breed certain small horses, under 14.2 hands, appear from time to time. These small horses are technically ponies but may produce

full-sized offspring when used for breeding, and they always have considerable value as children's mounts. Many such Saddlebred ponies were
and are from the finest bloodlines of the breed and registered with the
American Saddle Horse Breeders' Association. How many is not known because the registry does not list them separately, nor does it even record
their height.

In the early 1900s and thereafter the demand became so great for these
Saddlebred ponies that breeders in Kentucky and Tennessee where they
were principally found began to breed their best Saddle horses to ponies
just to get some smaller stock for children's ponies. Often Indian spotted
ponies of slight build, not the chunky type, were used for brood mares,
and thus for many years pinto-colored Saddle ponies were shown. We
still see them today. These were not registered, but no registration is required to show in a three- or five-gaited class.

Saddlebred pony classes are sanctioned by the American Horse Shows
Association under the Saddle Horse Division. They're particularly popular
today in Kentucky, Tennessee, and Missouri where almost every horse
show and fair have both saddle and fine harness events for these ponies.
In recent years Illinois and Ohio, also Alabama, Georgia, and other parts
of the South, in fact, wherever Saddle horses are popular, their little
brothers, the Saddlebred ponies, are right in there too.

They are turned out for the show ring just as the Saddle horse is, with
set tails, long toes, and weighted shoes. The youthful riders must be
properly dressed in saddle suits—Kentucky jodhpurs with matching riding
coat and a derby for daytime competition, formal tuxedo saddle suit with
silk hat for evening competition.

Since all Saddlebred ponies require a considerable amount of time in
the part of a professional to train, they become high-priced animals even
though they are used only by children and only in amateur stakes. A good,
finished five-gaited pony is worth up to $5000, even more for an outstand-
ing one. They change hands quite frequently, for when the child outgrows
the pony he or she acquires a horse in its place.

Though this is a pony, he is still a lot of animal, tending to have the
same high spirit and "go" of the Saddle horse. A beginner doesn't climb
into the saddle and take off, for these ponies are trained by signal to
perform, and something done inadvertently might cause serious consequences.

As previously mentioned, these ponies come in calico colors—white and
sorrel, white and black, etc. But for the most part they follow the regular
solid colors of the Saddle horse—bay, black, chestnut, sorrel, palomino—
and have the same white leg and face markings. In size they range from
13 to 14.2 hands. In conformation they are miniature Saddle horses, having

the same head refinement and long graceful neck, good chest and barrel, the superbly refined legs of flat bone, the high animation and alertness.

With its classic beauty, the Saddlebred pony has earned a spot in the show world that no other pony can touch, and it will be his just as long as youngsters come along who love the art of horsemanship at its finest.

The Walking Pony

The Walking pony is a branch of the Tennessee Walking horse family, a breed of pleasure and show horse which has, since World War II, become the most popular Saddle horse in our country.

Several reasons account for this.

He has smooth, almost tireless gaits and a wonderfully gentle disposition which makes him a real pleasure to ride and not a battle of tug and haul. He doesn't nip or kick down the stable out of sheer cussedness, and even if he hasn't been exercised for a few days he won't try to buck Junior or Grandma off his back. All of which makes him an ideal everybody's-horse.

He has three gaits: walk, running walk, and canter. In place of the wearying trot to which the rider has to post up and down, up and down at every stride, this horse's famous gait is the running walk, smooth enough for a rider to sip a glass of cider without a straw. Different from the pace which has a swaying lateral movement, different from the rack in which

Jimmie Ellis wins the World Championship Walking Pony stake at Shelbyville, Tennessee, in 1964 with his brilliant pony, Sun's Glory Boy.

the horse works his head from side to side, the running walk is a square, four-beat gait in which the rear foot overreaches the track of the front foot by from twelve to thirty inches. The horse, in performing it, nods his head up and down, which is why he's long been called a "Nodder." This counterweight movement takes most of the motion out of the back, resulting in a wonderfully slick, gliding sensation for the rider.

Walkers trace back one hundred and seventy-five years in Tennessee to the same old English imported stallions which helped found the Saddle horse. In addition, such early American stallions as Traveler, Tom Hal, Cockspur, Denmark, contributed much to the breed to fix its outstanding characteristic, the running walk. These smooth-gaited mounts have had great appeal ever since the colonial days for the country preacher and the country doctor making their rounds, the farmer or log-cabin mother riding into town with a basket of eggs. After the Reconstruction days they were known as Plantation horses, and any land owner who spent much time in the saddle owned one. In 1887 the Marshall County Fair in Tennessee had a Walking horse class with fifty-seven entries, attesting to their popularity.

So close was the Tennessee Walker to the Saddlebred in the early days that a versatile Walker often entered the Gaited classes at a show or fair. Roan Allen F-38, who died in 1930 and is considered a modern pillar of the breed, was one of the few seven-gaited horses the world has ever known. He could do the flat walk, the running walk, canter, a perfect square-trot, fox-trot, pace and rack, often competed and won in Walking Horse, Fine Harness, and Five-Gaited classes all at the same show.

Tennessee Walking ponies, like Saddlebred ponies, come out of the regular horse bloodlines of the breed and no distinction is made of them in the registry. Just as children in the same family will vary in size, so do horses, and when one comes along under 14.2 hands he is trained and used in Walking pony classes. Certain Walking horse bloodlines tend to produce smaller offspring than others, but no serious attempt has been made to isolate them and breed strictly Walking ponies.

Like his bigger brother the Walking horse, he is a solidly-built fellow with good shoulders, a barrel chest, short back, and strong hind quarters. Although the Saddle horse blood shows in his overall appearance, he doesn't have the same delicate refinement, but is an animal of more substance from dense leg bones to powerful body. His head is heavy-boned, the skull wide, and the upper lid of his eyes is often wrinkled. His movements glisten with style and rhythm, and when he shifts into his high-geared running walk, he whisks along, appearing to hug the ground.

Colorwise, he can be anything that can do the running walk. Black is the great show color, but he comes in sorrel, chestnut, all shades of roan,

This pony, owned by J. B. Floyd of Denison, Texas, is three-quarters Tennessee Walker and one-quarter Shetland. He is shown doing a good flat pleasure walk for Diana Floyd, the rider.

white, bay, brown, gray, palomino, even spotted, though these last are nearly always unregistered stock. His height as a pony is under 14.2 hands, but he seldom ever goes below 13 hands without being crossed.

The Walking pony is much easier to train than a Saddlebred. The running walk is so much an inherent characteristic that almost anyone can bring it out and develop it for pleasure riding with just a little effort. For show ring competition, more is required and here the hand of the professional usually enters in. Still, the Walking pony remains much less expensive than the Saddle pony, probably half the price on the average.

With the wave of popularity that has carried the Tennessee Walker into almost every part of the South and Midwest, even the Far West, Walking pony classes have become a fixture of nearly every Walking horse show program. At the Tennessee Walking Horse Celebration, the breed national championships held at Shelbyville, Tennessee, three major Walking pony classes are held—58″ and Under for Riders 15–18 Years Inclusive; 58″ and Under for Riders 14 and Under, and Walking Pony Championship of the World, 58″ and Under. This last stake is made up of the winners of the first two classes.

Only in rare instances have good Walking ponies been produced by outcrossing. The simple truth is that a special gait like the running walk tends to be a recessive trait and, when diluted by an outcross, is only partially retained. One of the few people who have been successful at producing crossbred Walking ponies is Mr. J. B. Floyd of Denison, Texas. By crossing a Shetland mare to a Walking stallion and then recrossing the female offspring back to Walking blood again, he has been able to produce a 14-hand pony with Saddle horse conformation, a fairly good flat walk, a running walk or fox-trot (a broken gait in which the pony walks with his front legs and trots with his rear legs, a surprisingly confortable combination), also endurance and vigor equal to that of most full-sized horses. These ponies make ideal mounts for small adults and elderly ladies who like to ride an easy-gaited horse.

In choosing his Shetland mares, Mr. Floyd is careful to pick out those with a tendency to saddle and says he has seen a few Shetlands that could do a pure running walk naturally. These would be the best, of course, and he adds that he has had no difficulty in the pony mare foaling from a horse. He uses a small, refined Walking stallion. The foal is influenced more by the dam than by the sire in this case, so its size is kept down further than if the cross were made Shetland stallion to Walking Horse mare.

The Walking pony has established himself as a pleasantly different star in both the pleasure riding and show ring worlds. As time goes by, his star is bound to rise higher and shine brighter, for he is that good a pony.

Chapter 11

The Icelandic Pony

New to America but ancient in its native land is the Icelandic pony, a sturdy, powerful animal with many interesting and unusual aspects to recommend him.

Historically, he has resided on the bleak and cold island of Iceland on the Arctic Circle between Greenland and Norway ever since Norsemen arrived from Scandinavia in 874 to settle. For the last eight hundred years no horses or ponies have been imported to Iceland, so the native pony is perhaps the purest in Europe. Today the island has around thirty-five thousand head, of which half roam free all year round.

The Icelandic pony is an exceedingly strong, compact animal, his head fairly heavy but well carried on a short neck and barrel chest. His short back, muscular hind quarters, and stout legs allow him to carry any adult with ease. Strong knees and hocks help too. With heavy mane and tail flowing, he's an attractive rascal as he moves along at a good clip, man or woman, boy or girl in the saddle.

An unusual aspect of the Icelandic pony is that he's the only known five-gaited Saddle horse in Europe. These are walk, trot, canter, pace, and running walk (called the *tolt* in Iceland). The *tolt* is a highly prized gait brought out by good training and horsemanship. The best gaited ponies are used for riding, the rest for draft work of all kinds from cartage to plowing.

Because of his surefootedness, strength, and range of comfortable gaits, the Icelandic is a fine trekking pony. In this very popular native sport, groups of riders travel cross-country through magnificent scenery, sleeping outside at night while their ponies graze on native pastures. During the day the ponies travel twenty-five to fifty miles, carrying men, women, and children safely and without fatigue.

The ponies stand generally from 13 to 14.2 hands. Lighter colors predomiate like sorrels and chestnuts. Other colors are palomino, white, brown, once in a while black and dun.

The first importation of the Icelandic pony to this country was in

1959 by Mr. Edward M. Crane, president of D. Van Nostrand Company. He saw several of the breed while on a trip to Iceland and was so taken by them that he imported four mares with foals to his farm in Red Bank, New Jersey, where they have done well.

However, the real start of the Icelandic pony in the United States came when the Lee Brothers of Alberta, Saskatchewan, imported three stallions and about seventy mares to Canada in 1959 and 1960. These ponies were dispersed at two auctions as well as at private sale in 1960 and 1961. Many came to the United States, particularly in the Colorado area.

Later, fifteen mares and one stallion were imported by George Williams of Boulder, Colorado. With this stock plus what had been brought down from Canada, the Icelandic Pony Club and Registry, Inc., located at Greeley, Colorado, was begun. At the present time, over a hundred ponies have been registered and more than twenty-five active members comprise the club. Some of these are breeders, but many just ride for pleasure in the Rockies and other beautiful but rugged spots of the West, and for this the Icelandic pony probably has no equal.

Because he's so good-natured, he makes a great pony for kids to learn to ride on, and he's been trained with ease to cut and work cattle proficiently on a couple of ranches in Colorado and Wyoming. This would seem to be a fine use for the pony, particularly by young people who want to train their own mount for this type of Western event. He has also competed successfully in Gymkhana events, especially those calling for speed and agility, like pole bending and barrel racing, and has been used in several 4-H projects.

Certainly no pony on earth is easier to keep than the Icelandic. If he requires no shelter on the Arctic Circle, he wouldn't want much more than a shed anywhere in this country. He can forage for himself and is naturally an easy keeper. Because of his fine disposition and powerful frame, he is a natural for children and adults both, particularly in cold and/or mountainous country.

Without a doubt his popularity will grow as more people discover him.

Chapter 12

The Crossbred

Although they are really not a breed, Crossbred ponies are looked upon almost as being so. Certainly one would have to call them a definite type, for they are small hunters in looks, character, and purpose. They do all the things that big hunters do in the field and at horse shows—not on a much smaller scale, either.

They go fox-hunting and follow the hounds over stone walls, ditches, hedges, and timber. They jump in pony hunter and junior hunter classes and have their own conformation classes at most of the major horse shows, particularly in the East.

The Crossbred pony ranges in height from 12 to 14.2 hands, but most are on the large size, being only an inch or two below the horse height. They are bred as intermediate hunters for children, hence that extra height is what gives them their purpose and makes them valuable.

A Crossbred is exactly what its name implies—a cross between two breeds, usually a small one and a large one, i.e., a pony and a horse, or more specifically a Welsh and a Thoroughbred. The parents don't necessarily have to be registered although it's nicer if they are. But using registered Thoroughbred mares in a Crossbred breeding program is rarely done. Such mares are bred to Thoroughbred stallions for race track prospects or for big hunters which go for a higher price than ponies. For the Thoroughbred side of the cross, a three-quarters or a seven-eighths mare will be used, which means that a grandparent or a great-grandparent was not a Thoroughbred, hence she can't be registered with the Jockey Club. Often hunter-type mares of horse size are used, and they serve well because they generally have good dispositions.

A Crossbred can also be a cross between two breeds of ponies. Some excellent results have been obtained, for example, by crossing Welsh and Hackneys. The offspring usually come out like small hunters around 13 hands, very flashy in looks and animation, and some can jump their heads off. Smokey Joe whose sire was the noted Hackney, King of the Mountains by the world famous King of the Plains, Hackney harness

champion, and whose dam was the Welsh mare, Belle of Wales, was champion hunter pony of the American Horse Shows Association for five years and seven times champion in his home state of Maryland. He's still going strong, though well into his teens.

Shetlands are seldom used for producing Crossbreds because they are too small. Welsh is the favorite pony blood. Connemara becomes increasingly popular each year. Dartmoor, Chincoteague, and Hackney blood is used from time to time.

Among the horse breeds, the Arabian and the Thoroughbred get the biggest play as stallions, while many grade mares around 15 hands are used.

There are many interesting aspects to the Crossbred business. A rather strong and constant demand persists for these ponies, but it would be a difficult, time-consuming, and costly job to make them into a breed. The situation is solved much easier by making the first cross and not going any further. What inevitably happens when you cross-breed is that the first generation has the qualities and looks of what you want, but by the laws of genetics, a high percentage of the second generation will throw back either to the father's or mother's side. Even when the quality offspring are chosen, a goodly percentage will not breed true.

Another point that makes for cross-breeding is that grade or unregistered mares can be bred to most any high quality stallion for a half or third of his regular stud fee.

Also, if you breed Welshes and come up with a mare of hunter type, she won't add much to your Welsh program but will be ideal for a Crossbred program. Same with a small Thoroughbred mare. Nobody on the track wants her, nor would a Thoroughbred breeder look with much glee upon her, but she's ideal for producing Crossbreds.

In halter classes at horse and pony shows, Crossbreds are judged on conformation, type, way of moving, and soundness. At a major show like Devon, classes are held for foals, yearlings, two-year-olds, brood mares, produce of Dam, Get of Sire, Champion Gelding or Stallion (most Crossbreds are gelded), and Champion mare. At Devon there is a special trophy for the best Crossbred Pony, Pennsylvania Bred, and this is almost always the largest class of the group, having twenty or more entries.

Crossbreds also dominate the pony hunter classes and competitions. One

This fine saddle pony, shown in an English Pleasure class, is an Arabian-Welsh Crossbred, Ala Arabi Radar, owned and ridden by Miss Kay Fiser of Burlington, Wisconsin.

Two Crossbred ponies and their youthful riders take a hurdle with perfect precision.

of the great pony shows of the country is the Maryland Pony Show held in July each year at Timonium. This four-day event has just about every class imaginable for hunter and jumping ponies.

The Crossbred also thrives at the Pony Rallies sponsored across the country by the United States Pony Clubs, Inc. At these rallies local Pony Clubs compete in dressage, cross-country and jumping events. The winning team of each region then goes to the national rally to compete there for the best in the nation. In these cross-country and jumping divisions the Crossbred is a natural.

In many parts of the country, particularly Virginia, Maryland, and the Carolinas, wherever point-to-point racing is popular, the programs usually include a junior event or two for youngsters under eighteen. This may be a flat race over the countryside, or a real point-to-point with more modest jumps than for adults.

Many women also ride the large-size Crossbred as a mount for fox-hunting. A small woman often finds a large mount difficult to maneuver, whereas on a small horse or a large pony she can execute the turns more cleanly and eliminate many of the problems that arise from the small rider and large horse combination. Her sense of balance and time is inevitably better on a 14.1 or 14.2 hunter; also, she has a greater feeling of confidence on a quick maneuvering, quick-to-recover pony than on a powerful mountain of horse flesh.

Crossbreds run the entire range of horse colors from black to white and pinto combinations. The regular hunter colors of bay, chestnut, and gray are the most popular, although youngsters love the piebalds and skewbalds. Though these have good hunter conformation, they have somewhere in their background a little Western cow pony to get the color mixture.

The price of a Crossbred depends pretty much on its "look" or conformation and its ability. Green broke, a young Crossbred can be had for $100 or a little more. A trained hunting and jumping pony will run between $300 and $1000. The higher you go, the better you get. They change hands often, just as quickly as children grow up, and certain stables deal almost exclusively in them. A little inquiring will uncover one with ease.

Chapter 13

Midget Ponies

For centuries men have been able to put ponies to practical as well as pleasurable use. Time and again their size and quality have been improved by selective breeding. Size has always had an important bearing on a pony's value. If he was too small in stature, he was essentially useless, so no one ever went out of his way to breed midget ponies. That is, until recently. Now in a few rarified circles, the smaller you can produce them the better—as long as they look pretty.

Midget ponies are pretty scarce animals. Only about one out of every five thousand ponies born qualifies, and it is this kind of odds that makes them worth up to $3000 each. By definition, a midget pony is one under 32 inches in height. Some say 36 inches, but the real dyed-in-the-wool "shortie" breeders draw the line firmly at 32 inches. No other limitations of any kind apply, though preferably they should have as good "horsy-looking" conformation as possible and not be pot-bellied or dwarfy. Midgets almost always have a lot of Shetland blood in them, hence come in the same range of colors—from solids and dapples to pintos. Also, for some inexplicable reason there are quite a few spotted midgets of Appaloosa patterning. This is not Shetland blood at all, but probably traces back to the small spotted circus ponies of Europe.

At the prices they command, midget ponies are pampered pets owned by those who like to have a tiny, conversation-piece of horse flesh around the house. They are small enough to be kept almost like a dog, and in some cases owners have taught them clever tricks such as lying down and playing dead. They are easily trained to ride and drive, quickly become a member of the family and, because of their size, require little space, feed, and upkeep. Though small, they aren't weak or sickly by any means, but, like all other ponies, have good strength and tough constitutions.

Until 1962 midget ponies never played a very prominent role in the horse world. Records occasionally tell of European royalty having one or two for palace children to play with. The most significant splash they ever made was in France during the 1850s and 1860s. Empress Eugénie, wife of

Napoleon III, had a special breed of miniature pony developed to pull her carriage around Paris. Like so many other fads feverishly pursued during the days of the Second Empire, the little fellows died out as a breed in a short while.

In the United States, midget Shetlands have come along from time to time but no one paid particular attention to them. American Shetland Pony Club records show that in 1888 Eli Elliot imported 140 head direct from the Shetland Islands. Among them was a 31-incher called Yum Yum who figured prominently in some of the early Shetland bloodlines. Many others have come and gone through the years without any great fanfare.

In 1962 all this changed, however. Señor Julio Cesar Falabella, a rancher outside of Buenos Aires, Argentina, sold some midgets to the Kennedy family and in the process gained enough notoriety to start a business of them. Actually, this strain of midgets was started by his grandfather in 1868 and improved by his father and himself. Today he has a herd of

This superb little fellow, about 30 inches, is straight from the Falabella ranch in Argentina. His near-perfect conformation is rare among midgets and a characteristic of Falabella's diminutive stock. Many midget ponies are spotted or Appaloosa colored as this one.

some four hundred head, the largest in the world, and he calls them midget horses rather than ponies although the strain was founded on Shetland blood. Several of Señor Falabella's are spotted or Appaloosa marked, as the excellent one shown in the photo on page 144.

Exclusive distributors for these little fellows in the United States, Canada, Mexico, Central America, and the West Indies is the Falabella Miniature Horse Farms, Inc., Scarborough-on-Hudson, New York. Current prices are $1500 for a gelding, $2000 for a mare, and $3000 for a stallion. Some of the purchasers have been David Sarnoff, President of NBC, Helmut Dantine, the actor, and Yul Brynner, who has two in Switzerland.

The largest American breeder of midgets is Mr. Smith McCoy of Roderfield, West Virginia, a grocery operator and former legislator who has a forty-head herd for a hobby. Naturally, his best pony is a 28½-inch stallion called The Real McCoy, but his most prized one is a 20-inch mare which is certainly one of the smallest of its kind in the world.

Mr. McCoy started ten years ago to collect and raise midgets. He went to a farm that had eleven hundred ponies and found four under the midget height requirement of 32 inches, then to a farm with eight hundred and found three. He finally got together about twenty-five which have now increased to forty despite several recent sales. Like all midgets, none are or can be registered. In color they range from red sorrel to dapple, black, and pinto.

The herd of Joseph Taylor of East McKeesport, Pennsylvania, is pretty much spotted. In fact, he advertises them as miniature Appaloosa ponies. All are under 36 inches, quite a few under 32 inches, some mature ones only 25 to 28 inches. Mr. Taylor's herd is built around a 33-inch POA stallion, Storm Cloud, purchased from the late Dr. F. B. Poling of Wichita, Kansas. Most of the foals are born solid-colored and gain their spots and blankets as yearlings. A system of breeding closely related individuals together is being used to fix the color, size, and conformation of the herd.

Dr. Marvin E. Hartley of Cambridge, Ohio, raises what he calls Miniature Shetlands. Mr. S. Watts Smyth of the Cross-U-Bar Ranch in Big Horn, Wyoming, has a herd of Midget Shetlands. In both cases they are one and the same, all under 36 inches, many under 32, the particular difference being in nomenclature.

Miss Jutta Schuman, a riding instructor at Rye, New York, imported from near her home in Germany some *Zwergpferde* or midget horses. They stand 8 to 10 hands (32 to 40 inches) and are supposed to have been carefully bred down from Arabian stallions and small mares in Germany and the Netherlands for coal mine work. Later they graduated to park shows, circuses, and nurseries and have now become fashionable family pets over there too.

Ten shorties from the midget herd of Smith McCoy of Roderfield, West Virginia, are tied to a hitching post to show their size and that of an average horse. Mr. Mc-Coy stands on the right holding a yardstick for height comparison. At left, Sugar-dumplings at 20 inches is undoubtedly one of the smallest horses or ponies in the world.

Miss Schuman trains them to drive in a *troika* or Russian three-horse hitch and finds they can pull up to five times their own weight. The *Zwergpferde,* she says, "are intelligent, easy to train, very gentle but spirited." They eat about a third of what a regular-sized horse does, anything from potato pealings to stale bread. Though these hard-to-pronounce animals may not be as small as most miniature ponies, they have splendid conformation.

Regarding the point of difference between midget horses and midget ponies, scientists say you do not distinguish between the species in this manner. A pony is a small horse, and midgets of the equine breed are bred down from small horses called ponies, not from large horses.

The true midget horse, i.e., born of regular-sized horses, is the dwarf which has been completely stunted in its growth. Take, for example, Tom Thumb, 23 inches, 45 pounds, eight years old and born in Mexico. Anyone can pick him up and hold him in their arms. His black-and-white pinto bride is called Cactus. She is 26 inches, 95 pounds, and twelve years old. Until recently they were part of an animal show owned by Charles Bertsch of Greenwich, New York, who exhibited them all over the East Coast at fairs and such. Both were found to be sterile by Cornell University, otherwise they would have been bred together. The result might have been a regular-sized horse. Now they reside with Arch McAskill in San Antonio, Texas, who has shown freak animals for forty years and deems Tom the smallest of his kind he has ever seen.

A dwarf horse has an entirely different look than a midget pony. Its eyes are oversized, its face extremely dished, lower jaw sometimes overshot. Its body is often a caricature of a horse, sometimes comic, sometimes pathetic in its deformation, whereas a midget is a well-proportioned miniature specimen of the species. This is not always achieved but it is the ideal, and certainly Señor Falabella's line of midgets is outstanding in this regard.

What often happens with midgets is that the owner becomes so enthralled with what he's got, he reports vital statistics with more enthusiasm than accuracy. Mr. McCoy has traveled thousands of miles to check out claims for tiny ponies. Recently, the Richmond *Times-Dispatch* told the story of Mae's Midget, a 20-inch peewee which weighed 20 pounds at birth. Off hurried Mr. McCoy only to discover it measured 31 inches when the yardstick was held properly. Still, it is a surprising midget.

So far, the market for midgets is not large, although there are plenty of people who would like to own one but who can't afford it. Some day, as more are produced, the prices may come down a bit, for the law of supply and demand applies even to the pony world.

The two dwarf horses standing under the Great Dane are Tom Thumb on the right (23 inches, 45 pounds) and Cactus on the left (26 inches, 95 pounds). They are part of a side show formerly owned by Charles Bertsch of Greenwich, New York, and now the property of Arch McAskill of Texas. Both were found to be sterile by Cornell University veterinarians.

Chapter 14

The New Forest, Dartmoor, Norwegian Dun, Miniature Donkey, and Burro

There are several worthwhile breeds which while not too numerous in this country, nonetheless have their avid followers. There are many other interesting breeds of ponies that roam different parts of the world, but by necessity we must restrict this book to those seen in the United States.

The New Forest Pony

As a result of importations in recent years, this well-known English pony seems destined to get off on a popularity spin like so many other breeds since World War II. It hasn't quite happened, mainly because an American club and registry haven't been formed, but there are signs of effort in this direction.

New Forest is a pretty old place. It was named that in 1079 when William the Conqueror took over its 66,000 acres for his private shooting preserve. Though it is still Crown land, more than two-thirds of it is open for grazing cattle and ponies as long as they stay within its boundaries. When they stray outside, they are impounded and the owners pay a fine. Automobile roads lace the forest, but for the most part the ponies are contained by grids at the exits. An estimated fifteen hundred run all year in the forest.

The origin of this pony is rather obscure. It is thought to trace back to the same source as the Exmoor pony, the ancient native pony of England. Through the years all sorts of blood have been introduced, from mountain and moorland ponies of kindred breeds to horses. In 1765 Marske, the 14.2-hand Thoroughbred sire of the immortal English racer Eclipse, was used in the Forest for half a guinea per mare. In 1853

Queen Victoria sent in a gray Arab stallion called Zorah who left his mark. Despite this, the New Forest remains a firm and easily recognizable type of pony, strengthened during the past thirty years by eliminating just about all the outcrossing.

The New Forest Pony Breeding and Cattle Society, formed in 1910, holds a show of stallions in the spring. A series of halter classes and one riding class comprise the program. The best stallions are awarded premiums, and all have to pass inspection in order to be turned out in the forest for breeding. The show champion is confined in an enclosure for positive service to special mares, while others are allocated different districts by the society. Quite a few owners now keep stallions as private stud, and this has helped improve the breed remarkably in recent years.

In autumn come the annual pony drifts (drives) organized by the commoners who own all the ponies. Each is identified by private brand. All are driven into big corrals, the foals branded and the stallions removed until the following spring. Later on, the Society conducts a large sale of mares, foals, and young stock of all ages.

Lawnhill Lightning II, 14-hand New Forest hunter pony mare, is owned by Mr. Donald Carmichael of Chagrin Falls, Ohio; Miss Pat Wood up.

From running freely in the Forest, these ponies become extremely sure-footed around bogs and logs, rabbit holes and ditches. Because they graze near roads, they become immune to traffic. The majority make children's ponies although adults often ride them too, hence the New Forest is billed as a fine family pony. In England people tend to ride more for pleasure and less for competition than we do, thus a family pony serves an important function for them. New Forest ponies are exhibited with great success at all the major shows. Special point-to-point races are held for them on Boxing Day (the first weekday after Christmas) with events for youngsters and adults. And the rest of the year people ride their New Forest ponies for both pleasure and fox-hunting. They are enjoyable hacks, and can be taught jumping and pleasure driving. Because of their gentle dispositions, they train easily.

Several of the New Forest breed have been used as polo ponies, and often polo pony stallions are crossed with New Forest mares for this purpose.

In size the New Forest ranges from 12 to 14 hands, the most popular

Imported New Forest mare shows classic strength. Foal in rear will shed out gray. Ponies shown here with Mrs. Betty Galloway are part of the William Olmstead herd at Gloucester, Virginia.

height being 13.2. If turned out on good grazing pasture when young, they tend to grow a little higher. They may be of any color except piebald or skewbald. Browns and bright bays predominate, with a number having the eel stripe (a dark line down the back). In conformation they are medium-width ponies with good riding shoulders, deep chests, strong but not coarse legs, which make them ride more like a horse without the quick choppy "pony stride."

The first importations to this country were in the late 1950s by Mr. John Boyer of Hanover, Connecticut, and Miss Patricia Wood of Rockbridge, Ohio. Additional importations have been made by Mr. and Mrs. William Olmstead of Gloucester, Virginia, and others.

Recently I had the pleasure of seeing the Olmstead herd of New Forest ponies at the historic Purton Plantation overlooking the York River and only a stone's throw from the rendezvous of Pocahontas and Captain John Smith. As I leaned on the split rail fence, Jack Straw, the English champion and herd sire, came over inquisitively, followed by the mares and foals. They were a beautiful lot of ponies, strong of leg and back, with a touch of Arab refinement, and their good-natured temperament was apparent in every move.

There are about twenty owners and half a dozen breeders of New Forest ponies in this country. Plans are under way to form a club and registry. At the moment the ponies bred here in the United States can be registered only in the English registry for which Mrs. E. H. Parsons, Deeracres, Lymington, Hampshire, England, is the secretary.

New Forest ponies have become extremely popular on the Continent, particularly in Holland, Sweden, and Denmark, where they are being used as children's ponies and are making a good name for themselves at shows. The Dutch already have their own Society and Stud Book.

With a little more time and organization, the New Forest seems certain to join the ranks of American ponies as an attractive and safe hunting and all-purpose pony for children.

The Dartmoor

On the Highland moors of Devonshire (southwest England) runs a breed of sturdy pony called Dartmoor. These bushy-coated little fellows are hardy enough to withstand the eternal mist and rain, wind and storm which sweep in from the Atlantic and both channels, weather that would make short order of the likes of a thin-skinned Thoroughbred or Arabian. The farmers use these ponies to ride about on and for carts and carrying packs.

For many centuries they have been a part of the area, but in the last hundred years were victimized by too much crossbreeding. Welsh, Exmoor, Fell ponies have all been bred into them, but worse of all Thoroughbred and Arabian blood has weakened the tough qualities of the breed. They average 11.2 to 12 hands in height, with 12.2 being the limit for registration. Traditionally they are dark-colored, being bay, brown, black, sometimes gray, rarely chestnut or dun. White markings, other than on the face, usually are a sign of Welsh blood.

These powerful little animals have solid, high-crested necks, small heads with little spike ears. Their bull shoulders and short backs are especially suited for carrying weight, as are their well-muscled hind quarters and stout legs. These ponies can really rough it. In winter their shaggy buffalo coats shed water like an oilskin, and with their streaming manes and tails and bushy forelocks that almost cover the face, they have a wind-blown look of a truly native animal, the raw, exquisite ruggedness forged by the hand of Nature. You know by looking at them that, were they left alone, they could survive forever, whereas the slick, man-made horses and ponies would die out within a decade if they had to forage for themselves.

The largest breeder of Dartmoor ponies in the United States is Mrs. Joan Mackay-Smith of White Post, Virginia. She has had a herd for some twenty-five years, bred them straight and crossed them to obtain very fine hunting and children's ponies. Offspring from her stock are scattered up and down the Eastern seaboard.

Canada has more Dartmoors than we do. Several hundred have been imported, most of them being crossed with Shetland blood for use as child's ponies.

The Dartmoor Pony Society, located at Pearroc Vean, Buckfast, South Devon, England, maintains a registry for purebreds and urges farmers and moorsmen to breed only registered stock. At last it would appear that the crossbreeding, so prolific through the years, is gradually being eliminated in favor of the more valuable purebred stock.

The Norwegian Dun

One of the truest representatives of the horse in a very early form is the Norwegian Dun. This quiet, mannerly little fellow of around 14 hands looks as though he might have stepped right out of time two thousand years ago. And indeed, he may well be a remnant of the true dun type of horse or Celtic pony which prevailed in northern Europe and Russia in prehistoric times.

A proof of this is that he always appears in the same color—dun or sand —and he always has black trimmings. This means black mane and tail, black slash down the back and black lower legs, sometimes with cross or zebra stripes on the thighs. Being around 14 hands, short-backed and chunky in conformation, he has the appearance of what scientists believe is a close facsimile of one branch of ancient *equus*. But don't think for a moment he's an old-fashioned-looking pony. Far from it! His dun and black tones form a color combination that no interior decorator could improve on, and he's a flashy little guy in movement and manner.

In Norway he works as a cart, pack, and riding horse in and around the fjords, which comprise one of the roughest landscapes in the world. Extreme sure-footedness, strength, durability, and a wonderfully gentle disposition are his forte.

In the United States he is scattered far and wide, popping up here and there when least expected. For many years the Broadmore Hotel in Colorado Springs had a six-pony hitch of Norwegian Duns which carried an old Western stage to and from the station, but urban progress squeezed them out. Some dude ranches in Colorado, Wyoming, and Montana use them for fun horses and especially for children to learn riding, for they are almost foolproof in this respect.

The only breeder I know of is Rear Admiral Robert C. Lee of Blairstown, New Jersey. He raises these interesting and exceedingly good-natured ponies for pleasure, and they provide it.

The Miniature Donkey and Burro

Though neither the miniature donkey nor the burro are ponies, it would be unfair to omit these cute and clever beasts of burden who for the first time in their centuries-old careers have finally struck it rich. They had to come to the United States to do it, of course, but now they live a fat and sassy way of life as pets, stealing the hearts of young and old alike.

To clarify a point at the start, there is a difference between miniature donkeys and burros. Miniature donkeys come from the Mediterranean part of the world (chiefly the islands of Sicily and Sardinia), range from 28 to 38 inches in height. The burro comes from Mexico, stands 40 to 50 inches high. Both belong to the Ass family which inhabited Asia and particularly Africa.

Miniature donkeys with their long ears, sad contemplative eyes, and bushy coats do not deserve the unbelievably hard work required of them since the dawn of history. In their native countries they bring in crops, draw wagons full of charcoal, carry huge loads of brush mounded so high and wide as to be hidden except for their slender trotting legs. They turn primitive mills to grind grain, pull cartloads of people to carnivals and

Registered miniature Mediterranean donkey jenny and twelve-hour-old daughter show the characteristic dark-trimmed ears and cross at withers and down the back. These belong to Danby Farm, Omaha, Nebraska.

Miniature donkeys are wonderful and absolutely safe pets for children. Here Wendy, Mary, and Bobby Mairs of Pasadena, California, have theirs hitched to a jog cart.

celebrations. A Sicilian or Sardinian peasant who owns three donkeys, even three miniatures, is a rich man. There is also a larger size, but peasants like the tiny beasts because they eat less and Americans like them because they make such gentle and affectionate and unusual pets.

They come in every shade of gray and beige, from a very light pearl-gray through a reddish brown to a dark chocolate that is almost black, but their famous trademark, the cross on the back, is always visible. The body of the cross starts in the stubby mane and goes to the tip of the tail; the arms of the cross bisect it at the withers, forming a most unique marking. Legend says that this is their reward for having carried Mary to Bethlehem and Jesus into Jerusalem.

Miniature donkeys' ears are usually dark-edged and white inside with a little reddish-brown at the base, and always ridiculously long, which gives them much of their humor. The female is called jenny or jennet, the males are jacks. They live a long time, too—thirty years is not a bit unusual.

Their great advantage around children is that they have no panic button whatsoever. If they want to get rid of a rider they don't buck him off or rub him off against a fence. They just sit down like a dog and perforce the rider slides off. Anyone can handle them. Also, they can withstand extreme heat and cold without inconvenience, are amazingly sound and require very little attention, all of which probably accounts for why they have had such a rough life wherever they went. I remember seeing them in Turkey carrying loads twice their own weight. Always they were treated with contempt (one of the favorite ways of swearing is to call someone a donkey), yet they did their jobs with unflagging effort.

In the United States these little fellows are trained to ride and drive at about one year of age. In winter they eat a quart of grain in the morning and a handful of hay morning and evening, but when pastures are green, they're reluctant to bother with the grain. They can be fed for fourteen to eighteen cents a day when there is no grass.

A Miniature Donkey Registry was organized in 1958 to preserve the race of purebred donkeys. The registry maintains an official stud book; each enrolled donkey has an official certificate and a number which is tattooed in his upper lip for permanent identification. Board members include Daniel Langfeld, Sr. and Jr., of Omaha, Nebraska, and August A. Busch, Jr., of St. Louis, owner of the St. Louis Cardinals and top man at Anheuser-Busch, also until his recent demise, Powell Crosley, Jr., of Cincinnati and South Carolina, owner of the Cincinnati Reds. The first miniature donkeys brought here from the Mediterranean area are believed to have been imported by Mr. Busch's father. The Langfelds bought their first one from him, a gelding for their cerebral-palsied daughter who learned to drive it with such ease that her parents were struck by the idea of raising them.

They bought more from Mr. Busch as breeding stock, picked up some others around the Middle West, and now maintain one of the largest herds in the country, between 100 and 150 at all times.

The registry restricts the height to 38 inches and under. These are not runts in any way but breed absolutely true to size and type. Importing them is now just about impossible because of restrictions. Sad-looking but joyful-acting, the little fellows are popular with grandparents who have grandchildren visiting them in the summer; with people who like them as curiosities; with people who fall in love with their solemn faces and long flagging ears and have them around just as pets. They learn to open doors, come into the house and lie down on the carpet, and they provide endless and safe fun for children.

Seventy-five years ago burros were known throughout the West as the miner's helper. Originally they came with the Spanish to Mexico. Today many are kept throughout the southern and central parts of the United States for raising mules and hinnies. Like the miniature donkey, the female burro or ass is called a jenny, the male a jack. When a jack is crossed with a mare horse, the result is a mule, a most useful farm animal. When a jenny is crossed with a stallion horse, a hinny is produced, an animal which resembles the mule physically but lacks its endurance, strength, and intelligence, and is just about useless. Both mules and hinnies are hybrids which cannot reproduce.

Burros, like mules, are widely used as work animals, are noted for their endurance, freedom from disease, sure-footedness, instinctive wisdom, and freedom from harmful nervousness. Their milk is often used in cases of consumption and dyspepsia. Like mules also, burros consume less food for a given amount of work than horses and thrive under rough conditions that a horse could not survive. They don't need to be fussed over as a horse does and they almost never harm themselves by overeating or drinking when too warm. The gestation period of a burro is twelve and a half months.

In Mexico the burro is the main beast of burden for transporting farm goods to market, carrying wood, ore, and the like, pumping water. A few years ago when burros became popular as pets, so many were shipped to the United States that the Mexican government finally in 1960 banned their export in order to keep the price within the means of the Mexican peasant farmer.

Here in this country burros are still used by ranchers and an occasional grizzly old prospector as pack animals, also for breeding mules and extensively for children's pets because of their gentle and affectionate natures. Now they survive here mainly through the efforts of a few widely scattered breeders.

Rare white burro has a pink cast to his coloring. A shade larger than the miniature donkeys, he will grow to about 40 inches. He is owned by Mrs. Vera S. McClure of Columbus, Mississippi.

Two such breeders are Mr. and Mrs. John Hood of Douglas, Arizona, and it's interesting how they got started. A few years back they bought a small ranch outside of Douglas, only to discover that the wells were equipped with burro pumps—the only means of pumping water. They had great difficulty finding burros in this area where they had once been plentiful. To prevent extinction of these animals, they bought up enough to start a small herd. Their burros range in color from various shades of gray to red-rust and black. Interestingly, some are pinto in color, and they are being bred to obtain more of these. The lighter colors have the characteristic cross running down the back and across the withers.

In Columbus, Mississippi, Mrs. Vera S. McClure raises white burros as does Mrs. Mary Ann Black of Newport, Tennessee. Snow-white burros are a rare type that came into the country when so many were being trucked in from Mexico before the export ban went into effect. They are not albino freaks but have dark gray skin and dark eyes. Occasionally a dark hair is found in their manes or tails, otherwise they are snow-white. They average about 40 inches in height and weigh 400 pounds. The young are not always born white but usually shed out to be so; sometimes a foal is born a beautiful soft shade of pink.

But regardless of color or size, these ancient animals, which have worked their way through history harder than any other, still possess their qualities of gentleness and affection, just as they did thirty-three hundred years ago when depicted in bas relief on Egyptian friezes, wearing their crosses even then. Their cross seems to have been more the burden of drudgery and abuse from mankind rather than any reward of merit. But at long last they have found a land which appreciates them for what they are, and as a result they have brought happiness to young and old alike.

Chapter 15

Trotting Ponies

Certainly no phase of the pony world has grown faster in the last few years than racing trotters. One of the chief reasons for this—and a wonderful part of the sport—is that it has been organized on an amateur basis. Thus, whole families, men, women, boys, girls, can participate, and the result has been a tumultuous mushrooming in all directions. A mighty big sentence is required to tell the story:

In approximately fifteen years, pony trotting has grown from scratch to an estimated two-million-dollar business involving three to four thousand ponies at close to a hundred licensed tracks across the country, at county and state fairs, complete with judges, timers, racing secretaries, owners, drivers, breeders, claiming races, stakes, futurities, racing silks, champions, world champions, and theories.

Nor has the tide of pony trotting anywhere near reached its crest. On the contrary, all indications are that it will expand to three or four times its present size in another decade or so and become the People's Sport just as the trotting horse was fifty to seventy-five years ago.

Pony racing commenced a few years after World War II when trotting horses began pricing themselves out of the amateur market. In scattered spots like Maryland, Pennsylvania, and Indiana, veteran trotting men who had ponies began toying with the idea of using them for fun racing because they were so much cheaper and easier to train.

About the earliest and certainly the most successful promotion of this idea was done in Maine by Howard Small, an inveterate pony breeder who runs a harness shop in Yarmouth. Beginning around 1950, several of the Down-East fairs, traditionally famous for their trotting horses, experienced difficulty in getting Standardbreds to compete. The big-time, big-purse raceways, which sprang into being after World War II, drained the trotting horses away from the county fair tracks. Some sort of trotting competition was necessary to please the summer crowds, and Small, realizing this, offered to put on a pony trotting exhibition. It went over so big that fair officials asked for more. The first full program, staged and pre-

A trotting-pony owner pays his entry fee and obtains a head number which is his badge for admission to the race.

sented in a manner comparable to harness horses, occurred at Cumberland, Maine, Fair in September 1952.

For the next couple of years Small promoted harness pony racing all over New England, putting on pony trots at any and every fair that would let him. In some cases, crowds up to ten thousand witnessed the races, and he credits much of the early success and amateur character of the sport to the widespread interest made by his "racing girls." Small's nine-year-old daughter, Jane, an accomplished rider and driver, along with several cute classmates, trained his ponies and drove them in the races against all comers. Their success was outstanding.

In the mid-1950s the Penn-Mar Circuit for trotting ponies was formed when the Mountainview Raceway at Frederick, Maryland, home of the

Maryland Pony Trotters Association, and the Twin Maples Pony Raceway at East Berlin, Pennsylvania, home of the Pennsylvania Pony Breeders Association, joined forces. A short time later the Conewago Raceway and the York-Adams Pony Trotting Association came in, and the Penn-Mar Circuit became one, if not the biggest, pony trotting group in the country. Meanwhile, tracks had sprung up in Massachusetts, New York, Ohio, Indiana, Illinois, and pony racing was off to a good start.

In the 1950s the pony market enjoyed an unprecedented boom. Good Shetlands were bringing up to $5000 a head, champions $10,000 and up; Captain Topper brought $56,500 at public auction. Some went even higher at private sale. Pony breeders were too prosperous to conceive that pony racing could develop into a family recreation and spectator sport as well as a valuable market for ponies. When the roadster pony gained a place in major shows, some breeders began to give speed a more prominent place in their breeding programs.

The softening of our economy in 1958 and an oversupply of small ponies caused all pony prices to tumble. There was no market for the quantities of small ponies which had been produced, and everyone realized the boom had been artificially caused by breeders buying to build up their herds, not due to a proportionate expansion of new users and followers. The sport of pony trotting, now in its infancy, began to use hundreds of ponies and proved a great outlet for all pony breeds. In a way, these deflated pony prices helped the new sport immensely by supplying well-trained harness ponies at cheap prices for all those who wanted to get started. Not all of them were good, but at least they provided fun and incentive. Pony racing spread to areas where harness horse racing had never caught on. Clubs formed into associations. Pony tracks were built. Rules were drawn up.

Some of the people who played an active role in the early development of pony racing in various areas are: Frank Clark, Oxford, Massachusetts; G. R. Burrier, Frederick, Maryland; Earl Sheaffer, Mechanicsburg, Pennsylvania (who won the first race for a purse greater than $3500 with his trotting Shetland, Moonlight Cloud); Ralph Trimble, Anderson, Indiana; Leon Clark, Martinsville, Indiana; Henry C. Meyer, Chicago, Illinois; Mrs. John Chapman and daughter, Becky, of Paris, France, and Medomak, Maine.

In need of a national organization, Howard Small organized the United States Pony Trotting Association, Inc., in 1960. Its purpose is to promote pony racing, license ponies, keep records, and establish a trotting pony registry. In setting up his early races, Small handicapped trotting ponies according to size, and this became the pattern for racing in the USPTA which has a 50-inch height maximum (to keep out small Standardbreds)

Trotting ponies come into position behind the starting car to begin a race. Starting car gradually accelerates its speed until it crosses the starting line, whereupon the wings are folded and it quickly drives off the track.

and two other divisions, Under 46-inch class and Under 43-inch class.

In 1964 the USPTA licensed over one hundred meets from Maine to Washington, and moved its main office to Lafayette, Indiana, under a working agreement with the American Shetland Pony Club. The association continues as a separate corporation with Howard I. Small of Yarmouth, Maine, as president and William R. Burns of Lafayette, Indiana, as executive vice-president.

USPTA rules generally follow those of the Standardbred except for the height classifications, and this has become a big issue in pony racing. Many feel that speed rather than height should be used to classify trotting ponies, otherwise the few top ponies of each height category will dominate the sport.

Sulkies are upended for safety, and ponies wait patiently for trotting to get under way.

Because of this and other factors, the National Trotting Pony Association, Inc., in Hanover, Pennsylvania, was organized in March 1964 by H. C. Clark of Ivor, Virginia, John J. McNamara, Philomont, Virginia, William Simpson of Baraboo, Wisconsin, Mrs. Sidney Swett, Unionville, Pennsylvania, Donald R. Moul, Abbottstown, Pennsylvania, Mr. and Mrs. Roger Scherff and George Gingell, all of Maryland. The Standardbred racing rules are used almost to a letter. Ponies must be 50 inches or under and be able to trot a half-mile in 2:20 or better in order to qualify to race. A pony may win two heats in times faster than his class limit before he is moved to the next higher class. A pony out of the money for four consecutive heats is automatically set back to the next slower class. A pony dropped back to a slower class is allowed one win in times faster than his class limit before he is reassigned to the higher class. Thus height has no bearing on the classification of a trotting pony in the NTPA. Apparently trotting pony owners prefer this system, for in just a short while the NTPA has grown by leaps and bounds.

From the beginning, betting and gambling have played little or no role in pony trotting. For one reason, when trotting ponies start competing against Standardbreds at the pari-mutuels they may be barred from the many Standardbred tracks they now race on purely as a self-protective measure. At this point the Standardbred and pony folk get along famously. The trotting horse people scratch their heads in benign amusement when the pony people come swarming into a track. The pony people don't mind. They just harness up, go out, and trot up a storm—and have a whale of a good time.

Second, most everybody wants to keep pony racing an amateur sport. In this way any family can have a couple of trotting ponies, a trailer,

Meteor Magic, holder of many trotting-pony records, first of his breed to officially break 1:30 for the half mile, going 1:29 2/5 on a half-mile track against time and without a prompter. Note the excellent conformation of this trotting pony which comes from the finest Shetland show blood. He is being driven by his owner, Howard Small of Yarmouth, Maine.

and take off for the races every weekend. It's not unusual for several members of a family—Dad, Mom, Junior, Sis—all to drive ponies on an afternoon card. If they have a good pony, they can more than make expenses, also bring home some cups and ribbons for the mantel, in the process of having fun.

Third, many fraternal organizations and religious groups, Protestant and Catholic, sponsor pony racing and have even helped tracks get started. They recognize not only the good, wholesome character of the sport, but also that it is an exciting release for youthful energy.

Most pony racing, except for two-year-olds, is for half-mile distances. Tracks built for pony racing and training in the past few years are quarter-mile in length. They are ideal for spectators because the ponies go around twice and you see more of them, but they are tough for setting records. Most county fair tracks are half-milers, and these are a little better because of the longer straightaway, but the going is often tougher.

Coming into the home stretch, trotting ponies are bunched up in an anybody's race. Note that the two women in the field are well positioned. In fact, No. 4, Duke Sweet, owned by Victoria Newman of Long Island and driven by Jane Plante, won this race, with No. 5, Kengo, driven by fifteen-year-old Barry Watson, second.

In several states pony racing has supplanted horse racing as the major grandstand attraction at county fairs. In 1964 trotting ponies raced at twenty-two fairs in Indiana, sixteen in Illinois, several in California, Washington, and Oregon, as well as at tracks and fairs up and down the whole East Coast. This fair trend favoring ponies is bound to continue as long as the raceways keep paying large purses which attract all the quality harness horses. Because purses are secondary to the pony racing enthusiast, most any progressive fair can stage first-class pony trotting events on a modest budget. And the crowd always loves them.

At some small tracks ponies race for trophies and ribbons only. There are quite a few races for purses in excess of $500 and some stakes for $1000 or more. Some breed organizations, notably the American Shetland Pony Club, have established stake events to promote their own breeds. The three-year-old American Shetland Stakes should be worth close to $10,000 in 1965. Races for $25,000 are predicted by 1968. Already a "Petite Hambletonian" of pony harness racing is being held annually at Trotterdale track in Randall, New York. Pony racing fans from all over the country attend, many as participants.

As purses increase, so do the value of trotting ponies. The following chart from the United States Pony Trotting Association, Inc., Rule Book shows speed per size of pony:

Height	Superior Time	Good Time	Certified Time
50″	1:33 ½ mile	1:45 ½ mile	1:50 ½ mile
49″	1:38 ½ mile	1:48 ½ mile	1:54 ½ mile
48″	1:45 ½ mile	1:54 ½ mile	2:00 ½ mile
47″	1:50 ½ mile	1:58 ½ mile	2:04 ½ mile
46″	1:54 ½ mile	2:04 ½ mile	2:08 ½ mile
45″	1:56 ½ mile	2:06 ½ mile	2:10 ½ mile
44″	1:58 ½ mile	2:08 ½ mile	2:12 ½ mile
43″	2:00 ½ mile	2:10 ½ mile	2:14 ½ mile
42″	2:06 ½ mile	2:12 ½ mile	2:16 ½ mile
41″	2:10 ½ mile	2:14 ½ mile	2:18 ½ mile

Those ponies rated "Certified" would be worth $400 to $1000, depending upon age, sex, and breeding. Those rated "Good" would be worth $600 to $1250. Those rated "Superior" would be worth from $1000 to $2000. Those faster than "Superior" would be worth considerably more, depending again upon their age, sex, and breeding. A few of the great trotting ponies are insured for over $25,000. Ponies suitable for racing may be bought for $250 on up to several thousand dollars.

Except for the height ratings, as previously mentioned, rules for trotting ponies closely follow those of the Standardbred which have been in operation for some seventy-five years. The age of a pony is reckoned from the first day of January of the year of foaling. A starting gate is generally used. Drivers must all be licensed. Usually two heats decide a race. Purse money, unless otherwise specified, is divided 45, 25, 15, 10, and 5 percent. Thus a good trotting pony can make himself two to three thousand dollars a year at this stage of the sport's development.

As previously stated most races are for a half-mile. But two-year-olds are encouraged to race no more than ¼ or ⅜ and never more than ½ mile. Ponies under 43 inches are also recommended ¼ and ⅜ of a mile distances.

The USPTA also has a planning guide of rules and tips for laying out a regulation quarter-mile track. It includes Judges' Stand, Grandstand, barns, 20-inch hub rail, and all dimensions.

Charlaus Madonna Racey, champion registered Welsh trotting pony, is warmed up for a race at Devon, Pennsylvania, by owner-driver John J. McNamara of Philomont, Virginia. Note the tremendous stride of this pony moving in the typically Welsh floating manner.

Many and varied have been the bloodlines of the trotting ponies. Probably 75 percent are grade or crossbred. Hackney blood has been most influential, but it needs to be diluted. The best cross seems to be Hackney-Shetland-Welsh or Hackney-Shetland. From it all a definite breed is growing. Small Standardbreds and Standardbred crosses are banned from pony racing. The Standardbred is no beauty and only coarsens the pony when crossed in. Most ponies are really beautiful and could win in an average pony show, so why lose this quality? Also, this is one of the points which pleases spectators so much. They love to see a dappled gray going full tilt with white mane and tail flying, or a pretty palomino, or a bay with the white socks of the Hackney.

Because of the sport's comparative infancy, only a few ponies may be purchased that have two parents that have performed in certified time. To date no great mare strains have arisen, and this is essentially what makes a breed. However, in the short span of pony racing several outstanding individuals have appeared that are destined to leave their mark.

All pony times are indicated in minutes, seconds, and fifths of seconds, followed by the size of the track, either QMT or HMT, quarter-mile track or half-mile track. Quarter-mile pony tracks are measured two feet from the hub rail; half-mile tracks three feet from the rail because most were designed for harness horse racing and the sulkies are that much wider. Ponies, except real small ones, usually negotiate a half-mile track approximately four seconds faster than a quarter-mile track.

Here are some of the outstanding trotting ponies to date:

Meteor Magic, by Meteor Cody who was four times National Champion Harness Shetland, ex Sky-way Magic. White reg. Shetland stallion owned by Howard Small, Maine, first USPTA pony to beat 1:30 for the half-mile —1:29⅖ HMT and 1:34 ⅕ QMT.

Charlau's Madonna Racey, by Monarch's Delight ex Severn Wren. Gray reg. Welsh stallion owned by J. McNamara, Virginia—1:32 ⅖ QMT.

Curtiss Big Noise, by X-Dangerous Dan ex Curtiss Elizabeth. Black reg. Shetland Stallion owned by J. McNamara, Virginia—1:32 ⅖ QMT.

Copper Lady, sorrel grade mare, owned by J. McNamara—1:32 ⅕ QMT.

Miss Petite, by Hob Nob Swell (reg. Hackney champ. show pony) ex grade Shetland mare. Won 68 times in 75 starts, owned by H. Small, Maine.

High Command, grade gelding owned by H. Durham, Bridgeton, New Jersey, driven by sixteen-year-old Robin Durham—world's record 1:26 ⅘ QMT.

Chester Good, grade stallion, owned by Doyle McKinney of Olney, Illinois—1:31 HMT.

King D, Shetland sire, Hackney-Welsh dam, owned by Daniel Lemler of Bourbon, Indiana—1:30 ⅗ HMT.

Shenandoah Lancer, reg. Welsh stallion, owned by Mrs. Jean Shanholtz of Damascus, Maryland—1:36 QMT.

Royal Flash, grade mare, owned by Donald R. Moul, Abbottstown, Pennsylvania—1:37 ⅖ QMT.

Duke (Pacer), grade stallion owned by Charles Lebo, Abbottstown, Pennsylvania—1:25 HMT.

Chief Counsel, Welsh-Hackney crossbred, owned by William Swomley of Frederick, Maryland—1:33 ⅗ QMT.

Black Magic, grade gelding owned by O. Harry Eure, Gates, North Carolina—1:31 ⅗ QMT.

Smokey Boy, grade gelding owned by H. C. Clark, Ivor, Virginia—1:32 ⅖ QMT.

Bean Blossom, calico grade mare owned by C. F. Maynard of Muncie, Indiana—1:32 HMT.

Three of the fastest trotting ponies in the business barrel down the homestretch at Rolling Meadows raceway at Philomont, Virginia. On right Curtiss Big Noise (1:32 2/5 QMT), a registered Shetland being driven by Richard Wartluft, is challenged by Charlaus Madonna Racey (1:32 2/5 QMT), a registered Welsh driven by John J. McNamara. Both are stallions. In the slot is Copper Lady (1:32 1/5 QMT) being driven by Bud May; she is one of the fastest mares racing today.

Pacers are beginning to show up within the ranks of the trotting ponies. They are usually two or three seconds faster than trotters, and the NTPA is to have special races for pacers in the very near future. Some tracks require that they be free-legged; others permit hopples.

Women have played a key role in pony racing since its inception. They have their own special races, and they get out and drive like the devil against the men in many events. One reason that they do particularly well (Small's daughter, now Mrs. Jane Plante, is the country's leading race driver with over 250 wins) is that they are lighter in weight than men, and weight is bound to make a difference with ponies. That is, when all other factors are equal, which they never are.

But pony races are usually nip-and-tuck affairs. Unlike the Indian-file finishes one sees so often at harness horse tracks, well-classified ponies race in a bunched field with two or three ponies often out as far as the third lane. Most pony drivers, especially those on quarter-mile tracks, race from wire to wire, as the stamina of ponies allows them to go the entire half-mile at close to peak speed. Quarter-mile racing strategy calls for getting to the front of the pack as early in the race as possible.

At this point, there is great variation among ponies, timewise, due mainly to training procedures and rigging. Those who condition their ponies best generally get to the wire first. Then rigging the pony, which means harnessing and shoeing him properly, putting on the right boots and hanging quarter boots correctly, is an art that few amateurs know. But because ponies have a great amount of natural "trot" in them, real speed and competitive spirit, they are considered to be equal to or ahead of the Standardbred at the same stage of development.

The advantages of ponies for harness racing are multifold. They can be kept in a much smaller area than a trotting horse, eat much less feed, train with much less effort and expense ($50–80 per month for board and training with a professional). They are not so unwieldy to handle, hence safer to have around, and they're easily transported in a pony trailer, which can be hitched to the back of almost any car. Above all, people old and young love to associate with a friendly, colorful pony. If the little fellow can go all out and win for them in competition, he steals their hearts forever.

All these factors go to make pony racing the attractive, exciting pastime it is. If its amateur character can be maintained, it certainly seems destined to become a national sport for both spectators and participants alike.

Chapter 16

Chariot Racing, Chuck Wagon Racing, and Pony Hitches

The Old West of gold rushes and smoking six-shooters is gone forever, but many of its traditions and customs linger in our midst apart from the TV screen. In recent years some of these have come to involve the pony world.

It was not too many decades ago that teamsters and mule skinners played an important role in the development of commerce and transportation throughout the West. They drove stagecoaches and ore wagons of two-, four-, and six-horse hitches, wheat reapers of 10-, 12-, and 16-horse hitches. Driving was a profession known and admired by real horsemen. It took a lot of skill to manipulate a four- or six-horse hitch through narrow streets and around sharp bends. The men who did this driving were a proud bunch whom the mechanical age forced to change but who never relinquished their love for the long leather lines.

From this background has come a series of driving sports involving teams of ponies rather than teams of horses, because once again ponies prove to be more practical in every respect. They're smaller, hence cheaper and easier to transport and at the same time require as much skill, if not more, to drive, for they're quick in all movements, dig in hard and pull with all the determination of their bigger counterpart, the horse.

For fifty years or more, pony hitches have been popular throughout the United States and used for advertising, parades, or the like, but it is in the Pacific Northwest that they have recently caught on as a sport and in competitive driving events. After World War II, many old-time teamsters took up pony hitches and today driving events are held at most of the fairs and pony shows in the Northwest. Beyond mere driving skill,

these events require the best in harness, wagons, decorations, and fast ponies.

These driving events divide into three groups—chariot racing with po-nies, chuck wagon racing with ponies, and four- and six-pony hitches. All are wild and wooly sports in the best Western tradition. Their amazing growth has come about because they are both great crowd-pleasing and participating sports. Ranks of the drivers swelled because of the excitement of the competition, and access to fairs and expositions was gained because they are colorful exhibitions that add spectacularly to the festivities. Everything grew because of the prize money offered.

Each year now world championships are held at Spokane, Washington. For the finals in 1964 some seventy-six contestants came from all over the western half of the United States and Canada. Nearly two hundred ponies raced, with a total value of livestock and equipment including char-iots, wagons, trucks, and trailers estimated at $350,000.

The sport is conducted under rigid rules. All equipment and harness is officially inspected for safety reasons; health of ponies is checked too. Drivers, before they can race, must pass a test and be issued licenses good for one year. Contestants must pass the same requirements again the following year. Thus mishaps are kept to a bare minimum.

Chariot racing is not really a sport of the old West, but rather a natural result of driving enthusiasm. It traces back to Greek, Roman, and Persian times and today carries with it all the colorful dress and traditions of the past. Charioteers include young drivers as well as old-timers, even some women. They wear flowing mantles and helmets and ride in brightly-colored chariots.

Chariot racing is done on a quarter-mile track with standing starts the method for beginning. There are three height divisions—Under 43 Inches, Over 43 to 46 Inches, and Over 46 to 50 Inches. A series of heats is run and a point system used to determine the eventual winners—five points for first, four for second, three for third. These are added up at the end of the meet, and the high-scoring driver wins. Each morning a drawing is held to see how the drivers will run against each other that day and what their lineup positions will be.

Bloodlines behind these chariot ponies are fantastic. Owners cross every conceivable type and breed to get what they think will be the swiftest. Owners try to match their teams as best as possible for color and conformation, but speed always remains the basic ingredient. Conditioning of these ponies is vitally important.

Chuck wagon racing is another rugged sport that has drawn avid followers from all over the Pacific Northwest and Western Canada. Here two teams come roaring around the bend for home as the "cook" in the rear of the wagon hangs on for his life.

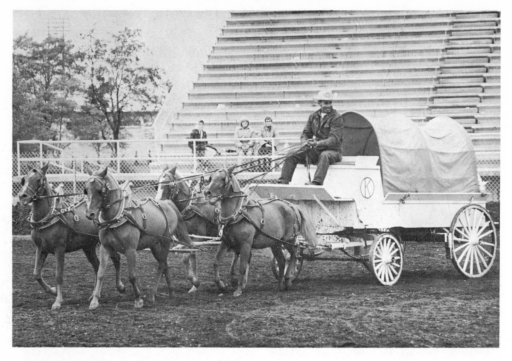

A beautifully matched four-pony hitch. Note the superb harness and immaculate wagon which can also be used for chuck wagon racing.

Chuck wagon racing is the fastest growing sport in the Northwest. Canadian racing rules and some American variations have been put together to form one of the nuttiest fun sports ever to come out of the West. Three teams of ponies hitched to suitable wagons are run at one time. Each team consists of four head strung out in two pairs. "Suitable wagons" means the canvas-top kind used in early roundups.

Each wagon has a driver and a cook. After they have lined up in the arena, the cook must set up his stove at the back of the wagon and go to the lead team and hold the off pony. When the gun goes off, the cook runs to the back of the wagon, folds up the stove, loads it into the wagon, jumps aboard himself and hangs on for his life.

The chuck wagon shoots off, full tilt, and makes a figure-8 around two barrels. Each team has its own set. After completing the figure-8, the three chuck wagons tear around one lap of a quarter-mile track and race back over the finish line. But that isn't the end. The cook must jump out of the back of the wagon, haul out his stove, set it up and light it. The first one to get smoke out of his stove wins.

This is a real clown race for the grandstanders to watch and great fun for all who participate. Anything can happen and usually does. Sometimes the stove or the cook tumble out en route, or the matches just won't light at the critical moment and the team that was last across the finish line becomes the winner.

Two other popular driving events and the ones from which the others really developed, are the Four- and Six-Pony Hitches. These are not so untamed as the first two but tend to be on the more traditional side and serve as a test of driving skill. Judging is done on conformation and uniformity of ponies, neatness of turnout which means harness and wagon, and ability to drive.

For this, all teams are given thirty seconds to drive around the ring at will at a trot and show how they can handle their hitches. Then they line up in the center of the ring for inspection of ponies and turnout. Finally, on signal all drive again at will, but this time it's a free drive at a dead run. It lasts for ninety seconds, and no one knows where the other teams will go or how fast they will move. With twelve to fifteen hitches zooming around the ring at the same time, it certainly takes on the air of an old Frontier Days celebration.

As previously mentioned, these events are not only exciting for specta-

A six-pony hitch cuts a figure-8 at full speed. Real driving skill is required to put these fellows through their paces to advantage. The front pair of ponies is called "the leaders" or "lead team"; middle pair is the "swing team"; pair nearest to the drivers is the "wheelers" or "wheel team." A separate set of lines runs to each pair of ponies. Note feather plumes on poll of each pony.

tors to watch but also great for old-timers who still have in their blood the love of driving long hitches at different speeds and with dexterity. Ponies in these exhibitions serve the purpose perfectly. Also adding to the incentive is prize money which often runs to $3000 or better per meet.

When old-time teamsters began to come out with their neatly painted chuck wagons, colorful six-up hitches and speedy chariots, it wasn't long before young faces crowded in with a galloping team of ponies and a handful of lines. Today the sport of driving has as many ruddy faces in it as leathery, weather-beaten ones, and they're just about as good on the lines, too.

Thus did the pony bring back driving in the Old West, and if his proselytes continue to multiply at the current rate, no doubt the Old West will take over the East.

Chapter 17

Buying a Pony

The preceding chapters have detailed the many facets of the pony world so that anyone interested in a certain use or breed of pony can follow up and buy one. An adult will favor a show or racing pony, a small child will love his short pony as a pal and for fun riding and driving, while a larger child will lean toward a hunting or jumping or Western using pony.

The problem in each case is the same: How do I find the pony to suit my needs and what do I look for? Answering these questions brings up others, such as the purpose of the pony, how will it be kept, age, disposition, etc. But before examining these issues, let's first settle an important point about ponies and children.

Some people feel that children learn to ride just as well on a quiet horse as on a pony. It's possible, but all factors being equal, experience proves the opposite. A child can manipulate a pony far better than a horse because the smaller animal is more suited to his size and strength. If he wants to speed up, as all kids do at some time or other, and flails his legs against the animal's sides, a horse will not go along as calmly as a pony usually will with such waggishness. Nor does the horse tolerate much hugging around the neck or pulling on the tail that most ponies accept undisturbed. Not all ponies are angels, but generally kids and ponies go together better than kids and horses.

Also, most children who own ponies have to take care of them, and this is certainly a much easier job in every respect than taking care of a horse. Rather than buying a horse or a large pony for a child to "grow into" it is much better to change animals as the child outgrows it. This isn't hard to do. Ads constantly appear in pony magazines to sell, buy, even exchange, because of this very reason. At the end of this chapter is a list of the important pony magazines that you will find useful. Subscribe to the one which covers the breed or area of your interest. The information, tips, suggestions they contain will be helpful in all phases of your pony's life.

Before buying a pony, you should attend some pony and horse shows

which have the kind of classes that interest you. Talk to the entrants afterward. Pony people are always a friendly, helpful lot who love to gas about their favorite pastime. Watch a model, roadster, or fine harness class, a pony race or pulling contest. Visit a breeding farm. Talk to trainers and dealers. Take in an auction or a production sale. There's one every week in some part of the country.

The first question in buying a pony is usually how much will I have to pay. That depends entirely upon the type and quality of the pony and how much training it's had. Fortunately for the buyer, pony prices have dropped considerably from their all-time high in 1957–8. They reached a low in 1963 and have begun to creep up again since then, but nothing in the neighborhood of the near-fantastic prices of the late 1950s.

To be specific, you can plan on paying $50 to $200 for a grade pony. At the lower figure he will be an untrained yearling, at the higher figure he should be a sound, riding pony. Good registered blood will run from $150 to $500. If it has show potential, it will start around $400 and run right on up. If it is a pony well trained for competition, perhaps even a winner in fine harness, roadster, jumping, trotting, or Western using, it will run from $750 to $3500 or more. Anything over $2500 would carry with it a recognized reputation and probably be a champion.

If you're a beginner, whether adult or child, you'll do better buying a trained pony the first time. If you can't afford this, find a good green one and train it yourself. It won't be too difficult. You must be twelve or older, and you'll need patience and the help of an adult, but we'll tell you how to do it.

An important consideration in buying a pony is its sex. In this regard, there are five categories from which one can buy a pony, and all have their merit. They are:

1. Stallion   2. Gelding   3. Mare   4. Mare in foal
5. Mare in foal with foal at side (This is called a Three-in-One package.)

Try your pony out before you buy him. If he is a show pony, put him in a show under actual competitive conditions and see how he reacts. Here a fine Welsh pony, Brays Island Delightful, owned by Dr. Charles Dubran of Sherburne, New York, and ridden by Jimmy Moss, is winning the Pleasure Championship stake at the National Welsh Pony Show, Devon, Pennsylvania.

People always wonder how safe stallions are. Many riding and driving ponies are stallions used and handled by children and women. Generally they are friendly and safe, but one must handle them positively. For a child's pet they are not recommended, but as a high quality harness show pony or trotter you will probably want one.

The gelding is the most gentle, reliable, and safe of all ponies, which is why he is altered. All children's male ponies are gelded, also most hunting and jumping ponies because they are in constant casual association with mares at fox hunts and horse shows.

The mare or female pony is always a delight to have around, is seldom nervous or highstrung, and makes an excellent fun riding pony as well as a fine performer.

A mare in foal is a quick way to get in the pony business. She can be ridden normally for the first six or seven months of her eleven-month gestation period and can be driven even longer.

If you buy a mare in foal with a foal at her side, you are in the pony business. But there is no prettier sight than a mare being ridden or driven and her youngster frisking along beside her. If it's a good one, you'll have people stopping you to buy it.

There are several sources from which you can purchase a pony. Let's examine the major ones:

Breeding farms

For every type of pony we have, there are breeders who always have stock of all ages and degrees of training for sale. They welcome visitors whether it's just to talk or as a potential customer, but it's best to make an appointment first. For the names and addresses of the breeders nearest you, write to the main offices of the breed of your interest, or look through the ads in the pony magazines. Breeders are reliable sellers because they have a reputation to maintain. You may not get a bargain, but you'll get you money's worth.

Trainers

In many parts of the country professional trainers make their livelihood by turning out and showing ponies. This runs the gamut from fine harness, roadster, and trotting ponies to hunters and jumpers. Very often a situation arises that forces an owner to dispose of a certain pony or perhaps his entire string, in which case a fine pony can be had at a reasonable price. Also, a trainer may know where just the right pony can be had for you. It's worth paying these men a reasonable fee to find a pony for you. They know their business and survive on satisfied customers.

Auctions

If you know something about ponies and their bloodlines, this is a good way to buy one. There are several types of auctions—the regular consignment sale to which anybody sends a few ponies to be sold; the annual national promotional sale which almost every breed now conducts and to which a prominent breeder usually consigns one outstanding pony; the annual production sale of large pony farms which breed many youngsters each year and dispose of their surplus in this way; the dispersal sale, which means a breeder is going out of business and selling everything— ponies, equipment, harness, trucks, trailers, etc.

All auctions are conducted in about the same manner. If it's a big sale, you get a catalogue listing and describing the ponies, their ages and bloodlines. You always have a chance to look the ponies over ahead of the actual sale, either the morning of the sale or the day before. This is the time to pick out those that interest you and note beside their numbers how high you might bid on each one. Then you go inside an arena or tent with seats or benches for the buyers and onlookers on one side, a runway or small ring in the middle and the auctioneer and his assistants on the other side.

A harness pony or roadster or jumper or gaited pony will be put through his paces in front of the crowd, his pedigree read and all pertinent information revealed about the animal. Of course, his strong points are accentuated and his weaknesses or blemishes played down in showmanship language, which slides over the head of the novice. If he is "serviceably sound" his body, legs, eyes, and wind are okay and he has no bad habits. "Legs go" means they are sound but may not look like much. If a pony is "chancy" it's a hint that he's a winner in disguise and you'd better not overlook buying him. If he's "goosey" he has a goose rump or a sloping croup. If he "stands a little careless" or "goes a little rough behind" it means he points a forefoot in the first instance, and has a spavin or the like in the second, making him "slightly" unsound. "A feather" or "a speck" or "a little bluish" in one eye indicates that he only sees well out of one eye. "Sold at the end of the halter" means no guarantee beyond ownership. This may refer to an "aged" mare, one which is only a broodmare and over ten years old.

Most auctioneers these days usually bear the title of Colonel. They conduct well-organized sales and don't try to hide anything, especially with ponies because they're always much sounder than horses. When you're at an auction, don't scratch your ear or stretch your arms during the hot bidding or you may end up with a pony you didn't expect. Auctions are exciting to attend, and with the quality stock which goes to the block these days you can buy in safety and with the assurance of getting your money's worth.

One important point to remember is that if you buy a pony at an auction, you must be prepared to get it home. Be sure to take at least a lead with you; a halter usually goes with the pony. If you didn't bring a trailer or truck, hunt around the grounds for someone with a public van and make arrangements for delivery. It's best to look into this beforehand so you know the cost and are also assured of a place.

A dispersal sale is a great time to buy tack and equipment that you need but can't afford to pay the new price for. Again, you have to be careful not to be carried away and bid too high. Be sure to inspect such items as harness, saddles, two-pony trailers, and pony vehicles carefully before they go on sale. Old leather or a rusted-out trailer isn't worth much and can't be repaired.

Local riding schools

This is an excellent way to buy a pony. The horsemen who manage these riding stables usually deal moderately in horses and ponies. Here you can try a pony as much as you like, and chances are that the stable manager will be honest in every way and stand behind whatever deal he proposes. He knows he has to live with you in the immediate area and can't afford to have you dissatisfied.

Advertisements

Many ponies are bought, sight-unseen, through correspondence as a result of an ad in a pony or horse magazine. They are usually satisfactory because the seller thoroughly describes the pony, stands behind his guarantee, sends photos and sells reasonably. He makes his money in volume sales, and the ponies are most always young stock which is no more than green-broken or only halter-broken. He will quote delivery costs right to your door. Another good way to locate a pony is through newspaper ads in your area. This way you can try out the pony and see how he acts before deciding.

IMPORTANT: If you buy a pony with registration papers, be certain they're in order before purchasing. Make sure you receive his papers with his transfer made valid to you when or before you pay for him. Don't be lax on this point!

Regardless of where or how you buy a pony, it will pay you to have a veterinarian check the pony to determine his physical soundness. This is

A good place to buy a pony is at a show. You can see how the pony performs and watch its temperament under noisy conditions. Here a fine Welsh broodmare and foal owned by Mr. and Mrs. Bohn C. Lindemann of Maidens, Virginia, wins a Section B halter class.

well worth the vet's fee, for he may find something you never thought of or noticed. Of course, this is impossible at an auction, but in every other situation it should be allowed. In case you don't or can't have a vet check, here are some things to look for.

Brush your hand at each eye and make sure the pony blinks. If he doesn't, he may be blind.

Lead the pony about and see how he acts. If he is to be a child's pony, he must be mannerly and calm, not restless or fiery. Best age for small children is from four to fifteen; a pony is settled and safe by then and usually not grumpy with old age. Pick up the pony's feet, handle him as much as possible. Let the child himself bridle and saddle the pony, mount it and put it through its paces. After it is warmed up, let the child take it for a short run to make certain it's not wind-broken (he will wheeze and roar if he is). Have the child put him back in his stall and see how he acts there.

The important point is to find a pony that fits the child. When mounted

If you buy a jumping pony, you should try it out thoroughly under several conditions first. This is Scot's Grey Captain, a champion POA gelding.

in the saddle, the child's legs shouldn't go below the belly line. Keep it above this if the child still has a lot of growing to do. To repeat, the important point is: *Have the pony fit the child.*

If it is a driving pony and you know what to look for, hitch him up and try him out in the ring or on the track. If you don't know or aren't quite sure, bring along someone who knows driving ponies, even if you have to pay him for his time.

When the pony is standing in a model pose, study his conformation and make sure his proportions are good. A short back is preferred for riding. A long-bodied or barreled pony is rough under saddle and will eat a lot, but generally makes a fine roadster or trotter.

A sharp- or high-withered pony is hard to keep a saddle on properly and harder to ride bareback. He is usually slab-sided, i.e., his ribs tend to be flat rather than rounded out naturally. There is also the other extreme, the pony with no withers at all and a back like a tabletop. A saddle on him spins around under his belly when the child tries to mount.

Also, the extremely wide-barreled pony is hard for the small child to manage because it spreads his legs so far apart he can't do much more than hang on.

Look at the pony's legs carefully—from the side, front, and rear. Faulty positions of the legs almost always lead to a defective way of going. If he is pigeon-toed (toes in), he will wing out when moved at a trot. If he is splay-footed (toes out), he will wing in at a trot, sometimes to the point of brushing the other leg. If he is knock-kneed, he will interfere; bow-legged, he will go wide at the knees. If he is buck-kneed, kneesprung, or over in the knee (all the same), he will be unstable and stumble a lot. With calf-knees he will have a pounding gait when ridden. Steep pasterns will make his stride short and stilty with too much concussion and not enough spring. The accompanying drawings show these and other major defects.

Cow-hocks are the same as knock-knees, only on the rear legs, and can easily be seen when standing behind the pony. They amount to the kiss of death in a show pony of almost any type, but some ponies can jump their heads off despite this fault.

Sickle-hocks are best seen from the side. The hocks are set too far behind the point of hip, which gives a sickle-look to the lower region of the rear legs. This is a serious fault in a show pony and not desirable in any pony.

The accompanying drawings also show the major bone, muscle, and ligament defects which cause unsoundness and impare the pony's looks and/or serviceability.

Fistula of the withers (not saddle sores) appears as a swelling in the withers region and may discharge pus. It's a difficult condition to treat and often leaves the animal stiff in the shoulders. A show boil or capped elbow is an enlargement of the bursa, caused usually by lying down in a stall without enough bedding. Over in the knee or kneesprung may be a congenital defect or may be caused by a tendon injury or inflammation of the knee joint. Young ponies will usually straighten up with proper care, but in an older pony it's more difficult, if not impossible, to cure.

Bowed tendon is a result of terrific strain or a blow. It can be caused by a bogged-down pony trying to jump out of mud or being ridden too hard too young. It is an enlargement of the flexor tendons and considered a serious defect. A splint is a bony growth along the cannon bone which can cause lameness until it sets, but ponies seldom get them. Sidebone, almost always in the forefeet, is a calcium deposit which causes lameness until it has hardened, but ponies have such good, tough feet that they are rarely bothered with this.

Bog spavins and bone spavins or "jacks" result from strains, sprains,

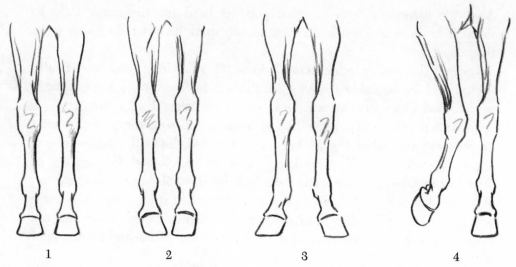

1   2   3   4

Above:

Front view of pony's front legs showing correct and faulty conformation: 1. shows correctly-formed front legs which are straight and true; 2. is pigeon-toed; 3. is splay-footed; 4. is winging out or paddling, an action typical of the pigeon-toed pony.

Below:

Major defects of pony's legs caused by faulty conformation: 1. buck-kneed; 2. calf-kneed; 3. sickle hocks; 4. cow-hocked.

Opposite:

Major defects of pony's legs caused by strain or injury: 1. bowed tendon; 2. quarter crack in hoof; 3. splints on front legs; 4. thoroughpin in the gaskin of the rear leg; 5. curb on the hock of the rear leg; 6. windpuff in the lower cannon and fetlock area of rear leg; 7. bone spavin in lower hock area of rear leg; 8. bog spavin in lower hock area of rear leg.

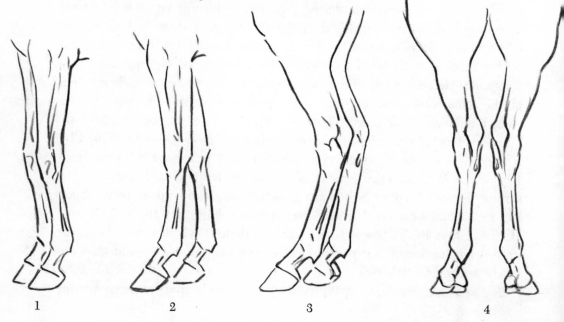

1   2   3   4

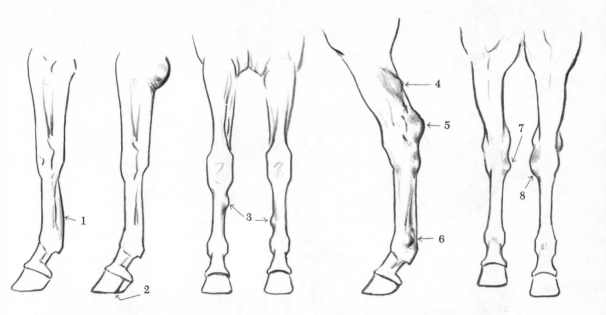

concussions, and faulty conformation, but they are seen much more frequently in horses than in ponies. Curb is an enlargement of the back side of the hock joint; thoroughpin is the straining of the rear flexor tendon and might be seen only in a pulling pony which exerts severe strain on his hind legs. Ringbone is a bony enlargement in the pastern area, resulting from a sprain, blow, or faulty nutrition, leads to permanent lameness but is seldom seen in ponies.

Quarter cracks and center cracks are fractures in the hoof wall and can cause a painful soreness. They are usually the result of dry feet or poor blacksmithing or too much concussion, especially when barefooted on hard surfaces like roads.

Ponies are very sound and tough animals. They seldom succumb to the above ailments. If you find any on a pony you are considering purchasing, it would be just as well to forget it and hunt up a sound one.

As far as age is concerned, you may find it a bit hard to tell a four- to ten-year-old pony, but if he's an old-timer you should be able to spot him with ease. He'll be a bit sway-back or down in the croup, probably both. His lower lip may hang loosely and there will be indentations at his temples. If you look at his teeth, they will be long and slanted, and the gums will have receded. Around the ninth year a dark line called Galvayne's Groove begins to extend downward on the upper corner teeth only. By the fifteenth year it is halfway down the upper corner teeth, and extends the full length at about twenty years. It disappears completely after the pony reaches thirty. The accompanying diagrams of teeth will help you distinguish a pony's age.

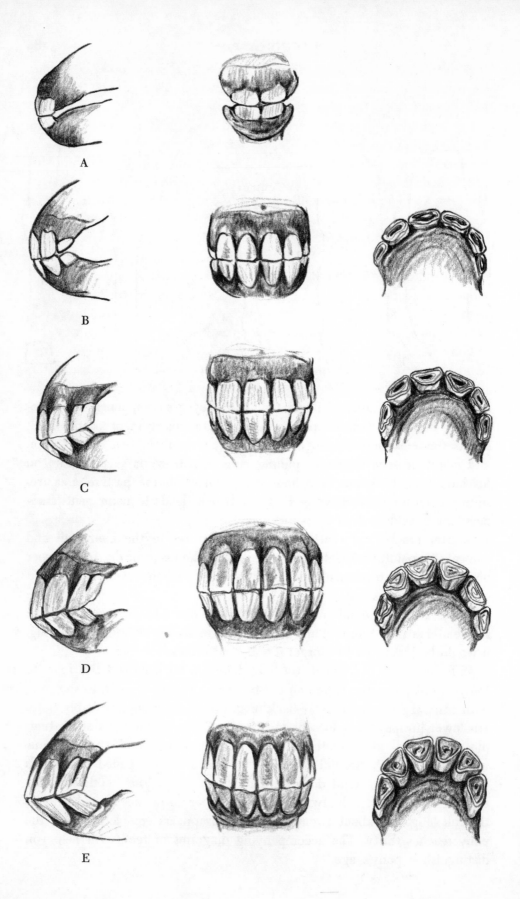

A

B

C

D

E

Remember also that after you have bought your pony, other costs must be considered, namely tack, food, and shelter. How much these cost will depend upon the type of pony.

For a child's riding pony, a saddle and bridle will be needed. A new English saddle can be bought for $50 and up, a new bridle or hackamore for $10 and up. A nice stamp-tooled Western saddle, imported from Mexico, is available for $40. A show or jumping saddle will run $100–200. For $600 you can get a magnificent new parade outfit inlaid with German silver. It includes a silver mounted saddle with ornate *tapaderos* to cover the stirrups, an elaborate breast collar and gleaming *serape* which drapes over the pony's loins halfway to the ground. Even the bridle is studded and coated with German silver. Less elaborate parade outfits are available for a quarter of this price. Used riding equipment can be had for a pony for $25 to $150, depending upon the make and condition of the saddle, but it must be good, otherwise you're better off buying new.

Pony show harness comes in different grades and ranges in price from about $50 to $150. This includes patent leather blinkers, patent leather girth, breast collar, and the works. A fun pony harness runs from $35 to $50. Harness for trotting ponies is $50 to $75. Stallion show tack runs around $50. Pony pair harness runs about $150. Heavy harness for pony hitches and pony pulling is around $200 per team.

To show a pony under harness requires a vehicle such as a viceroy or roadster cart. They run from $100 for a lightweight racing sulky to over $800 for the top-grade viceroy. Here is where you can hunt for used equipment and, if you can find it, save some money. Again, be sure to look it over carefully.

Cost of feeding and housing a pony depends upon what he will be used for. All ponies are tougher than horses. They like cold weather and can

Opposite:
The age of your pony is indicated by his teeth. With a little observing and practice, you can determine quite accurately the age of any pony. Milk teeth on a foal come in looking like those in ILLUSTRATION A. ILLUSTRATION B *shows the mouth of a four-year-old pony. The four front teeth are permanent ones, with only the milk teeth (baby teeth), which are smaller and whiter, remaining at the corners. The permanent teeth have well-defined cups as shown in the right-hand drawing.* ILLUSTRATION C *shows an eight-year-old pony mouth in which Galvayne's groove is just appearing in upper corner tooth, and cups are disappearing from lower corner teeth, after which time the pony is said to have a "smooth mouth." In the ten-year-old pony's mouth, shown in* ILLUSTRATION D, *the angle at which the teeth meet is becoming more acute, and Galvayne's groove shows prominently. Also, the cups have disappeared in the lower teeth and dental stars are appearing. In* ILLUSTRATION E, *a fifteen-year-old mouth, the teeth meet at quite an acute angle, and Galvayne's groove shows more than halfway on the upper corner tooth.*

rough it, but they must have some sort of shelter and a fenced pasture or paddock where they can exercise and possibly graze. You can't stake a pony out on a cow chain. You may get away with it for a while, but if a stray dog or the like frightens him, he'll either break his halter or injure himself, and there's always the threat of entanglement.

The shed for a fun pony need not be more than a three-sided building with a roof to provide protection against rain and snow. A show pony requires much more if he is to be kept in quality condition. This means a box stall and an area to work him properly. These facilities must be planned for in advance, and the cost will vary in different areas of the country. Housing and fencing for a fun pony shouldn't run more than $150, but for a show pony it will depend upon existing buildings which can be converted and utilized.

In spring, summer, and fall, if your pasture is reasonably good, there's little need to give a pony grain unless he's being worked hard. He will consume, through the winter, about a ton of hay, and will need a little grain and always a salt lick. His feed bill will run in the neighborhood of $50 to $150 a year, depending upon local supply and price.

A show or racing pony requires more care than this, of course. They are grained most of the year round, and show ponies don't get the chance to load up on hay because they must keep their girlish figures. Naturally, the cost of maintenance is considerably higher.

Other essential items are pails, a blanket, and cleaning equipment ($15), a set of electric hair clippers ($45), and maybe one of the new pony grooming vacuum cleaners that are a whiz ($70). Also, there may be shoeing occasionally ($5–10) if you want to show, and once in a great while veterinary services.

Initial expenses will be more than the upkeep on a pony. Give him a chance and he'll pretty much take care of himself.

Here is a short review of the salient points to remember in buying a pony. They are listed in order of their importance.

CHILD'S RIDING PONY
1. Mannerly disposition
2. Does the rider fit the pony?
3. Is the pony sound (consider age and health)?
4. Conformation

FINE HARNESS AND MODEL PONY
1. Conformation
2. Way of going
3. Alertness or show presence

4. Soundness
5. Manners
6. Bloodlines

ROADSTER PONY

1. Way of going
2. Speed
3. Conformation
4. Manners
5. Soundness
6. Bloodlines

TROTTING PONY

1. Speed under actual racing conditions
2. Soundness
3. Stamina
4. Age
5. Manners
6. Conformation
7. Bloodlines

HUNTING AND JUMPING PONY

1. Mannerly disposition (not easily rattled)
2. Soundness
3. Jumping ability
4. Conformation
5. Bloodlines

WESTERN USING PONY

1. Mannerly disposition
2. Soundness
3. Performance ability (barrel racing, pole bending, flat racing, roping, cutting, etc.)
4. Conformation (including color, if applicable)
5. Bloodlines

The above is only a skeletal outline, but will give you something to go on.

Here are the pony breed directories and list of pony magazines mentioned earlier:

PONY BREED DIRECTORY

American Shetland Pony Club, Inc.
William R. Burns, Secty.-Treas.
Box 1250, Lafayette, Indiana

Shetland Pony Identification Bureau, Inc.
1108 Jackson Street, Omaha, Nebraska

American Hackney Horse Society
(registry for Hackney Pony)
Mrs. J. Macy Willets, Secty.
527 Madison Avenue, New York, N.Y.

Welsh Pony Society of America
Mrs. Sidney Swett, Secty., Unionville, Pa.

Pony of the Americas Club, Inc.
31 First Street, N. E., Mason City, Iowa

National Appaloosa Pony, Inc.
112 East 8 Street, Rochester, Indiana

The Americana Pony, Inc.
G. L. Booth, Secty.
421 State Bank Building, Winfield, Kansas

American Connemara Pony Society
Mrs. Bruce Read, Secty.
RFD #1, East Pepperell, Mass.

Galiceño Horse Breeders Association
711 People's Bank Building, Tyler, Texas

American Saddle Horse Breeders' Association
(Gaited Ponies) C. J. Cronan, Secty.
929 South 4 Street, Louisville, Kentucky

Tennessee Walking Horse Breeders' &
Exhibitors' Assn. of America (Walking Ponies)
H. Tom Fulton, Secty., Lewisburg, Tennessee

Icelandic Pony Club and Registry, Inc.
Mrs. Judith Hassed, Secty.
56 Alles Acres, Greeley, Colorado

United States Pony Trotting Association
  William R. Burns, Exec. Vice-Pres.
  Box 1250, Lafayette, Indiana

National Trotting Pony Association, Inc.
  Donald R. Moul, Exec. Secty.
  575 Broadway, Hanover, Pa.

United States Pony Clubs, Inc.
  Mrs. John Reidy, Secty.
  Pleasant Street
  Dover, Mass.

PONY MAGAZINES

American Shetland Pony Journal
(reports Shetland and USPTA news)
  Box 70, Aledo, Illinois

Your Pony
(reports on all pony breeds and NTPA news)
  Box 125, Baraboo, Wisconsin

Pony of the Americas Club Magazine
(reports on POA)
  31 First Street, N. E., Mason City, Iowa

Welsh News
(reports on the Welsh)
  Unionville, Pa.

The Chronicle of the Horse
(hunting and jumping pony news and show results)
  Middleburg, Virginia

The Western Horseman
(some pony articles and stories)
  3850 North Nevada Avenue, Colorado Springs, Colorado

Gaited and Walking ponies are covered respectively by:
Saddle and Bridle
  8011 Clayton Road, St. Louis, Mo.
Voice of Tennessee Walking Horse
  Box 3054, Chattanooga, Tenn.

The Americana and Galiceño have monthly news bulletins which are sent out to members.

Chapter 18

Care of the Pony

Keeping a pony means keeping him healthy. Though he is a tough and sturdy animal in every way, he still depends upon you for his entire existence. He won't require inordinate care but he will need daily attention. Just how much depends upon whether you live in the temperate South or the colder North, in the country where pasture is plentiful or in the suburbs where the pony will have to be stabled most of the time.

A few words of caution. Prepare for your pony before you buy him. Don't bring him home and then start building his paddock and stable. Also, remember to consider winter as well as summer in your planning. This may mean insulating a stall or locating a shed or feeder in a more protected place. Also, try to anticipate danger spots like protruding nails, loose wire, or access to the feed can, and eliminate them before they cause trouble. Let's start with the bare necessities. You can elaborate on them to suit your needs and your pocketbook.

Pasture or Paddock

Pasturing your pony will save on the feed bill and provide him with a place to exercise when not being used. Ponies love to run and cavort and roll. Minimum size of a pasture is 2–3 acres per pony. Remember to include a tree for shade during the long hot summers. Provide your pony with the best pasture possible for as much of the year as possible. If you seed a new pasture, talk over with your county agent what grasses will be most suitable—red top, timothy, alfalfa, Dutch clover. Yellow clover can be noxious because it contains dicoumarin which reduces the ability of the blood to clot and can cause serious, if not fatal, problems for a mare when foaling. Also, don't fertilize the pasture heavily with nitrate. The grass or alfalfa will grow fine, but the pony may become temporarily sterile or even die of nitrate poisoning.

The pasture must be securely enclosed by at least a four-foot-high fence. The best type is post-and-rail or split rail. Sheep hurdle and heavy wire fences are fine except that they won't take too much of the rubbing the pony will give them in the spring when he begins to shed his long winter coat. Never use a single-strand electrified fence or barbed wire as farmers use for cows; the results will be disastrous. The gate should be stout and wide, with a stock latch or chain to keep it securely closed.

The paddock is an exercise area for your pony to romp in if he doesn't have a pasture. It should be no less than 30 by 40 feet, enclosed by good fencing and arranged so his stall opens into it and he can come and go as he wishes. If you do any fence painting, be sure to use lead-free paint. Otherwise the pony can nibble himself into lead poisoning very easily.

Shed

If you pasture your pony all year round, you should erect a shed to give him some protection from rain and snow and wind. It's also a fine place for his salt, grain, and hay in the winter. After all the talk in earlier chapters on how tough ponies are and how they have lived in semiwild conditions for centuries, you may feel a shed isn't necessary. The difficulty with most ponies raised under rigorous outdoor conditions is that they develop the habit of slouching behind boulders, under trees, and elsewhere to a degree that affects their conformation. The same pony, raised under better, man-made conditions, is less likely to be cow-hocked or have too sloping a croup. Building a shed will be worth the effort for the pony's sake.

It should be no less than 10 feet deep and 12 feet long, have a pitched roof at least 6 feet high at its lowest point, and face south. It can be built of old lumber, even sawmill slabs, but use substantial posts at the four corners so the pony rubbing against it won't topple it. The corrugated metal roof should have any sharp, protruding corners bent over.

Stable

Most ponies kept in or near towns and cities will be stabled for lack of more room. This calls for a box stall with a dutch door opening into a paddock. The stall can either be a separate building or part of a barn, garage, or the like. The Department of Agriculture has excellent plans for a pony barn. Easy-to-assemble prefabs can be bought. A tool shed or chicken coop can even be converted.

Opposite:
Pony fencing for paddock or pasture is important. Shown are the four most popular types: 1. board fence; 2. split rail fence; 3. sheep hurdle fence; 4. chain-link wire fence.

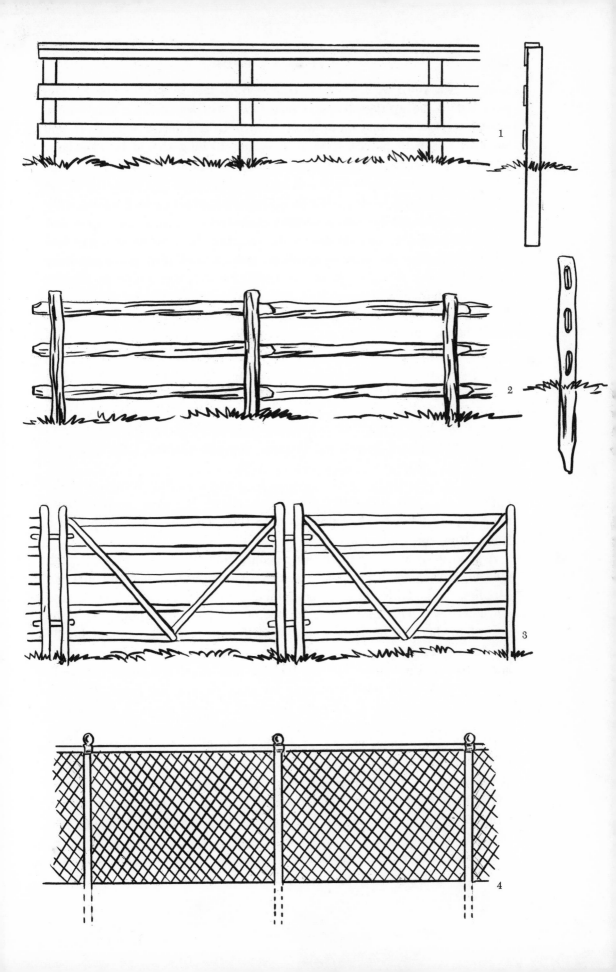

1

2

3

4

Whatever you use, it must be at least 8×8 feet inside; 10×10 will accommodate the average horse; 12×12 will take any horse. This is mentioned in case you may later want to switch to a larger animal. If you plan to stick with ponies, then 8×8 is fine. Ceiling should be at least 7 or 8 feet high, with a good big overhead light high up and out of the way. The main purpose of this light will be to allow you to groom your pony in his stall if you don't have any other protected area to use. Insulate walls and ceiling for winter and summer comfort.

The floor of the stall should be dirt or clay. If it becomes soggy and offensive smelling, it must be sprinkled with lime. If the dirt is sandy or full of very fine stone, so much the better for drainage purposes. Clay is sometimes hard to get, expensive, and doesn't drain well, yet is traditionally the horseman's favorite. Concrete floors are not satisfactory; they're cold, damp, and too hard on a pony's feet and legs. However, one of the best floors I ever saw was of poured concrete well-pitched to a drain; over it was placed a layer of 2×6 oak planks spaced ¾ of an inch apart like duck boards. The boards eliminated dampness and hardness, the gaps provided fine drainage for urine, and the stall could be disinfected and cleaned out with a hose whenever desired. The cracks had to be mucked out every couple of weeks, but the stall was the cleanest I ever saw. Of course, only straw bedding could be used.

When constructing a stall, it's wise to place a sliding window on the opposite side from the dutch door. This allows for cross ventilation on clear days or whenever the pony is not in his stall and helps keep everything drier and more fragrant.

A good dry room, adjoining but separate from the stall, must be available for storing feed, hay, tack, sulky or viceroy, grooming and first aid supplies, and stable-cleaning equipment (rake, pitchfork, broom, and wheelbarrow). This room *must* be out of reach of your pony, for if he noses into the feed bin, he'll gorge himself until he's sick, perhaps fatally so. Store grain in galvanized garbage cans with springs to keep lids on and rats out. Buy baled hay by the ton and stack it against one wall.

In the stall you'll need a manger for your pony to eat from. The old-fashioned iron manger is all right but hard to keep clean. A heavy-duty galvanized pail attached to a ring in the corner by a double-end snap is better. There are also special buckets shaped to fit a corner, with a bracket to hold them in place—very good for water. Don't use plastic buckets as ponies have a tough time digesting them! A hay rack is not necessary; just put the morning and evening allotment of hay in one corner. Attach a bracket containing a salt block to the wall high enough so the pony can comfortably reach it.

The dutch door should be four feet wide and seven feet high, the lower

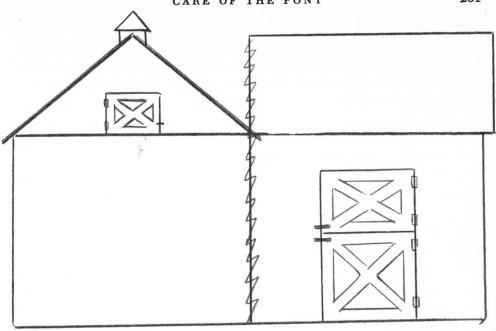

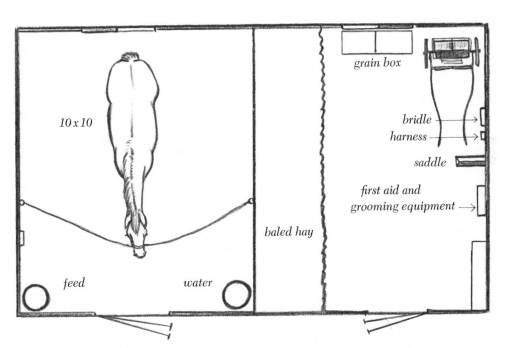

10 x 10

grain box

bridle →
harness →

saddle

first aid and
grooming equipment →

baled hay

feed   water

Stable layout for pony. A box stall should be 8'×8' minimum, preferably 10'×10', thus
allowing change to horse at a later date. In this case, feed and tack room is another
box stall which can be utilized if necessary. Front overhang to a barn is more convenient
for grooming, also more expensive in construction. Stable dutch door should be 7' high,
the lower part 4', the upper 3'; it should open into or be near the paddock.

half at a height so the pony can extend his head over it and have a look around. You'll want an outlet plug to run a set of clippers, and make all the wiring BX cable to be rat-proof, hence fireproof. Also, in the stall, put up two solid rings (not hooks) on opposite walls. You can snap into these and form cross-ties when you want to groom or clip your pony or clip his feet. Remember about painting—no lead-base paint where the pony can chew it.

For bedding, use wheat or oat straw, peat moss, wood chips, sugar-cane fiber or peanut shells. Never use hay because the pony will eat it, soiled or not. Make a good deep bed, three to five inches, and each day clean up all the droppings and soiled bedding with a barn shovel or five-tined pitchfork and toss it into a wheelbarrow or two-wheeled cart. Dump in a manure pile that is not in the paddock or adjacent to the stall because in the summer it will draw too many flies. Straw that has become damp can be dried out by placing outside in sunlight, fluffed with a pitch-fork and reused. Ponies tend to eat bedding of straw, so the other types are a little better in this respect but more expensive and harder to handle. Whatever is thrown out each day must be replaced and if for any reason the bedding becomes damp, throw it all out for fresh. A pony standing on soggy footing can easily acquire a hoof disease called thrush.

Feeding

The methods of feeding your pony will vary considerably, depending upon what you use him for and how hard you work him. The child's fun pony can be kept in excellent shape just grazing on pasture three-quarters of the year. Hay and a little grain the rest of the time will suffice. How-ever, if you have a harness or jumping pony, a trotter or any kind which is worked hard and really conditioned, he will require top-grade food and plenty of it. The pasture pony has little stamina.

Ponies love hay. It is good for them and keeps them occupied for long periods of time in the stall. Always make sure the hay is free of mold and dust, also poisonous sprays. Hay cut from or adjoining orchards which are sprayed heavily is too dangerous to feed. Each morning stalled po-nies should receive what they can clean up in about an hour. A little extra at night will keep them calm and occupied. Timothy mixed with alfalfa and a little clover makes about the best hay.

Among the grains, oats is the most popular for feeding ponies and is best digested when rolled. Bran makes a fine laxative and can be mixed one part with two parts of oats. Also, it can be fed as a hot mash once or twice a week simply by mixing with hot water in a bucket, stirring and letting set until cool before serving. Corn can be used in place of or with oats, although it is heavier and inclined to put weight on a pony, so 15 percent less should be fed. It should be cracked, or a mill can beat it up, ear and all, into a rough meal that mixes well with oats or bran. A little linseed meal serves as a good laxative and also helps bring out a fine coat.

In most areas you can buy well-balanced, prepared horse feeds in meal or pellet form which have the hay and grain all conveniently combined. They're a little more expensive but admirably suited for the hard-working pony, particularly the show pony which must keep a thin waistline and not have the big belly that comes from living on pasture grass and hay.

Conditioning the pony for competition is an art. Four to six months are required for a model or fine harness pony to reach top physical condition. Coming in from pasture, a pony needs a month or better to lose his grass potbelly. Best diet is prepared food with a little hay morning and night. As the pony fills out, he develops a fatty tissue which burns off under consistent harness or saddle training. This leaves his muscles good and hard. If he gets too lean, you have to increase his intake of food; if he remains a might chubby, cut down a little. Never change the diet or the amount suddenly. Regularity of routine produces results.

No formula can prescribe how much to feed a pony. You have to experiment and use common sense. If his droppings become hard and dry, he's constipated and needs a twice-a-week feeding of the hot bran mash previously described. If he's sluggish, increase his grain a little. If he's too lively and hard to handle, cut down on his feed. When the pony remains thin but eats plenty, check for worms or bad teeth. A simple filing or "floating" of his teeth by a veterinarian may be the remedy.

Don't ride or drive a pony immediately after he's been fed. If you have to work him out for any reason, cut his feed in half. If your pony is tired from a long ride or a hard fox hunt, don't give him a full feeding of grain. Give him half the usual amount and a little more hay. If your pony bolts his food, place a round, smooth rock five or six inches in diameter in his feed pail or manger. He will have to nuzzle the stone out of the way for each mouthful, which will slow down his eating.

Water is the cheapest and certainly one of the most important parts of your pony's diet. He should have a bucketful, clean and fresh, in his stall so he can have a sip *almost* whenever he feels like it. Note the word *almost!* When your pony comes in hot from a workout, even though you've walked him to cool him off, take his water bucket away and give it back to him an hour later. The only time a pony shouldn't have water is when he's hot; then he *really* shouldn't have it.

During winter in cold climates you can keep the water from freezing by placing a small electric heater in the pail. Try to maintain it at 40 degrees or better.

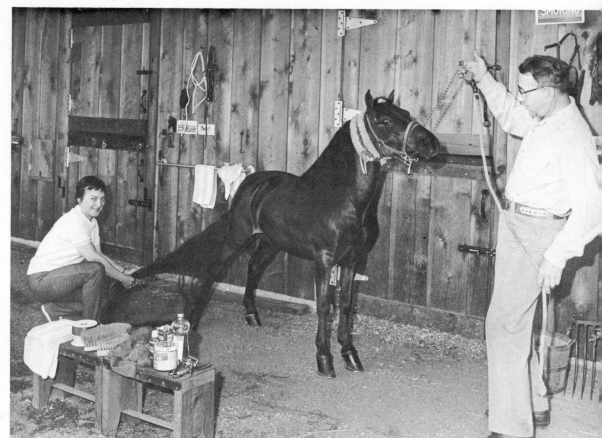

Grooming is especially important if you intend to show your pony. Here, Dr. and Mrs. Malcolm Teller of Maple Valley, Washington, prepare one of their Shetlands for showing. The pony is curried, brushed, and wiped off, mane and tail arranged by hand, not combed, hoofs cleaned and dressing applied to them. The jowl strap keeps the pony's neck from becoming too thick.

In hauling your pony off to a one- or two-day show, it is advisable to carry your own water so you don't have to use the local brand, whatever that may be. A change in water often throws a pony off his feed for a couple of days, and this can be disastrous at a show. Put a little baking soda in the drinking water a couple of times during the week before a show and use it every day you're at the show. This is a trick used by old-time horse and stock men.

Remember: Don't leave your pony in the stall without exercise. Cut down on his grain whenever you don't use him, and let him run in the paddock at least.

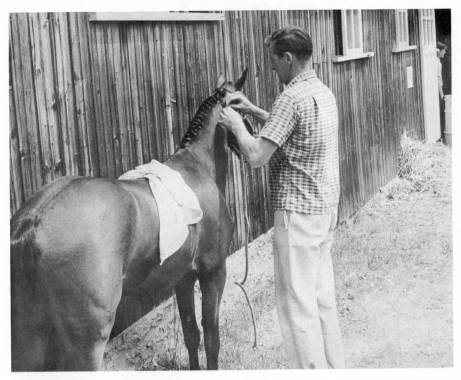

If your class requires that pony's mane be braided, be sure to do a good job of it.

Grooming

For health as well as appearance it's essential you keep your pony well groomed. Cleaning him gets rid of the body wastes exuded through the skin, helps his circulation and digestion. Grooming is particularly important to a pony because of his long bushy hair. Don't let it get matted, particularly in springtime.

To do the job, you need a dandy brush, a rubber curry comb, a body brush, a hoof pick, and a couple of cheap bath towels. You should also own mane and tail combs, a sweat scraper, a shedding blade, a body sponge, a tack sponge, and some saddle soap, all to be kept in a handy box that you can carry anyplace.

To groom your pony, secure him with cross-ties that snap to each side of his halter and keep his head steady. This is best done on a barn floor or leadway, but can be done right in the stall if the rings, mentioned earlier, are installed. You simply use two lead ropes as cross-ties. Start at the pony's head and work toward his tail. Use the wooden-backed dandy brush on his head, face, ears, and throatlatch, and on all the bony parts of his body like knees, hocks, and cannons. Then slip the curry comb into the left hand and the body brush into the right, and begin to curry

A hunting pony gets a new borium-tipped shoe. Note how well the frog has been shaped. Only under special conditions is it necessary to have ponies shod, but feet must be kept cleaned and trimmed at all times.

his neck, shoulder, and body on back to his tail with a two-handed action. As the curry comb loosens dirt, dandruff, and dead hair, the body brush wipes it away. To do the other side of the pony, walk around in front of him, not behind him. When you're finished, wipe him off with a towel, then comb out his mane and tail or brush them well with the dandy brush. A pony's mane should be trained to fall to the right side of his

Borium-tipped pony shoes as shown here not only last much longer but also provide excellent gripping surfaces for winter riding in snow and ice, also parade riding on hard-surfaced streets.

neck. Give his forelock a brushing too, then sponge out his nostrils, tail area, and sheath. To finish the job, brush a little hoof dressing onto each of his feet. It makes the hoofs look better and keeps them from cracking and splitting.

The fastest and probably best way to groom a pony is with a portable vacuum cleaner which has a curry-brush attached to the nozzle. A good job is done in half the time, and for a show pony it is certainly worth the investment.

Care of Feet

Grooming also includes keeping your pony's feet clean, which means raising each one and cleaning it out with a hoof pick. When you move around your pony and especially when you lift his feet, always talk to him and run your hand over his shoulder or flank so he knows where you are.

To raise a front foot, stand close to the pony, bend over and place your shoulder against his and actually lean against him a little so he shifts his weight to the other three legs. Then simply lift the leg and bend it bottom up and scratch out everything carefully around the frog and shoe if he is wearing one.

The hind feet are a little more difficult to lift, but use the same procedure. Place your shoulder against his hip and lean into him until he shifts his weight so you can pick up his hoof for cleaning. Most ponies are cooperative, but some are very touchy about their feet. It pays to find this out before you buy.

Caring for the feet of an unshod pony is most important. You need a farrier's knife, a pair of nippers, and a farrier's rasp. For the first time or two, a knowledgeable horseman should show you how to nip off the tough hoof, file it down level, and trim the frog. If you don't keep a pony's unshod feet trimmed and level, they will split and get all out of shape. Also, it is most important to keep the feet of foals and yearlings level and true. Uneven hoofs can turn their toes in or out to an extent that will effect a fast-growing young pony's legs. Fun ponies can be ridden safely without shoes but shouldn't be galloped on hard or frozen ground or pavement.

All competitive ponies, except those in model classes, need to be shod, and this is no job for the amateur. For the harness, roadster, or trotting pony, weighted shoes are imperative, and the style as well as the amount of weight is of the utmost importance. You will do best to rely upon professional help in making a selection. A pony's balance of gaits can be entirely changed by weighted shoeing; faults can be corrected or created. One basic rule is, don't apply the weight too young.

A hunting and jumping pony needs the regular type of shoe to protect his feet and keep from slipping in rough going. If a farrier won't come to your place for one pony, you may have to ride to him or to the nearest stable which he visits. Whether shod or not, a pony's feet should receive attention every six weeks.

After each hunt or workout, feet should be checked and cleaned. Stones often become wedged under the shoe, or the frog may be cut and need attention. In winter, a pony's foot can ball up with slushy snow which should be removed before stabling.

While on the subject of feet, thrush is a disease of the frog which comes from a lack of care. It amounts to rotting of the hoof because of dampness and neglect, and is easily recognized by the foul smell which accompanies it. First, clean out the hoof and apply one of the prepared remedies; then clean out the stall and *keep* it clean! Remember: Don't leave your pony in the stall without exercise. It's bad on his feet. Let him run in the paddock at least.

Clipping

With the approach of fall, your pony will begin to grow a thick bushy coat for winter protection. In some breeds it is heavier than others. You have a choice of clipping the pony after which you must keep a blanket on him and exercise him daily, or not clipping him which will prevent you from riding him very much because he will heat up quickly and be difficult to cool off. A pony with a winter coat should have the freedom of a paddock or pasture every day, and frequent grooming will not be necessary or possible. A clipped pony will have to stay in his stall most of the time and requires lunging, riding, or some kind of daily exercise. If it's cold, he can't be turned out for more than half an hour at a time.

Of course, a show pony must be clipped, also any other pony which is worked to any extent during the winter.

Clipping with electric clippers is not a tough job if your pony is used to it. If he fights you from fear of the buzzing noise, it will be a thankless job requiring the help of another person or two. Secure him with cross-ties as though you were going to groom him. Plug in the clippers and see how he takes to the sound. Talk to him and keep petting him. Start on a shoulder and work against the hair up the neck toward the head. If the pony is at all sensitive, leave his head until the end. Do his whole body, working always against the grain of the hair. Don't bother with his legs, but stop at his belly line, hunter-style.

If your pony is exceedingly nervous and begins to fight the operation, you'll need a friend to hold a twitch on him. This is a 12-inch piece of ³⁄₁₆ rope or leather run through a hole in the end of an old broom handle and knotted. The loop is slipped over the pony's upper lip and tightened until he becomes quiet and mannerly. Someone must hold the twitch while you clip. It doesn't hurt the pony, merely draws his attention away from what you're doing to the pinching on his lip. Blacksmiths couldn't work without them.

One thing to be careful of while clipping is not to burn the pony's skin. The clipper head will become extremely hot unless you stop occasionally and let it cool off. Dipping the blade into half an inch of kerosene helps both to cool and to lubricate it.

There are neat little plastic skids which you can attach to the clipper head to leave more hair. If you use a ¼-inch one you will have a ¼-inch of hair on your pony when you're finished and he'll be able to take the extreme cold a little better.

Your pony will start to shed out in early spring and look patchy. Don't clip him at this time as it will dull his new coat. Groom him vigorously, and use the shedding blade. This little gadget really pulls the dead hair out in a hurry.

In the way of blankets, you will need at least one good heavy winter one for a fun pony if he is clipped. In the spring you should wash it and store it in a box with some mothballs until the following fall. If you have a show pony of any type—harness, racing, jumping—you will also

need a sheet to use in chilly weather and also when you're walking him
to cool him out after a hard workout. A hot pony should always be lightly
covered so that drafts don't get to his body, and you should walk him
until his body is dry. You can best tell this by running your hand down
his neck and feeling his chest. If it's dry, you can safely put him back
in his stall.

There's a new anti-sweat sheet on the market made of heavy cotton
mesh. The air pockets are supposed to allow unhampered air circulation
and quick evaporation of all moisture. Used under a sheet, it's supposed
to give as much warmth as a heavy winter blanket. After a pony has been
exercised, this anti-sweat sheet can be put over him and he can be left
in the stall to dry out safely without being walked. So the claim is made,
but I can't vouch for it from experience.

Don't turn a pony loose in paddock or pasture with a sheet or blanket
on. He'll only roll and get it all mud or more likely tear it to pieces.

Bathing

Every once in a while you'll want to give your pony a bath, particularly
after a ride when his coat is stiff with dried sweat. If the weather is good
and warm, there's no reason not to do it, providing your pony is cooled
out and you *don't use cold water.*

You'll need three buckets of warm, almost hot water. Don't use water
from a hose unless you can adjust the temperature to almost hot. If you
use the three-pail system, make the first one mildly soapy—no strong de-
tergents. A human hair shampoo is too foamy; horse shampoos and body
washes are available.

Grab yourself the big body sponge and start in, covering neck, ears,
head, shoulders, back, legs, everything. Work fast and rub hard. Wash
out the sponge, and use the second pail of clear water to rinse off the
soap. You won't get it all off with that pail, but the third one should do
the job. Take your sweat scraper and scrape off as much loose water as
possible from neck, shoulders, back, and body. Don't scrape the legs or
any other bony part. When you've finished this, take a bath towel in each
hand and wipe the pony down, then walk him until he's dry.

After each ride you may not want to wash your pony completely down,
but you should rinse off the saddle sweat marks and around his poll
where the bridle crown rests, his eyes and nostrils, also his legs and belly
if they're muddy. This will save a lot of grooming later. Wash down a
pony's legs often. He'll like this and it's good for him. Keep half a dozen
bath towels on hand for rubbing down your pony. They're tops for this
and can be thrown in the washer for easy cleaning.

Wash your pony down with mild soap and warm water after a strenuous workout. Make sure it's a warm day, and don't let the pony stand in a breeze during or after washing.

Insects—Flies, Fleas and Lice, Ticks, Bee Stings

In every part of the country ponies are bothered by flies. A sorry sight is a pony in the heat of summer, stamping his feet, twitching his sides, slashing his tail, shaking his head in a vain attempt to drive away the endless flies which bite him until his legs and ears and face are bloody. In this day and age it is only a sign of neglect. There are completely effective fly repellants on the market—all sorts of sprays in bombs, washes which you can sponge over the whole body, sticks for eyes, ears, nose, and other sensitive areas, vaporizers which kill all insects in a stable, even a sugar bait for sprinkling on manure piles and other breeding areas.

If you have a hundred-pony herd at pasture there are effective fly chasers. Don't neglect your pony when fly time rolls around. His disposition will be much better for it.

Sometimes fleas and lice get into a pony's coat, particularly while in the pasture. When a pony starts rubbing up against fences, posts, boards, to scratch himself, you had better check him for flea or lice infestation. One treatment is to lunge your pony a little until he works up a light sweat, then wash him down with a mild solution of lysol and walk him dry. Another way is to get a good flea and lice powder from your veterinarian and sift it into the coat carefully, making sure it works down to the skin where these mites live and bite. If you don't attend the condition, the coat will soon be marred by big bare spots; also the flea or lice infested pony is difficult to keep in condition.

In certain parts of the country, ticks are a nuisance in ponies. After hibernating all winter in dead trees and the like, ticks appear in the spring and can be a pest through the summer. Ponies pick them up while being ridden through a forest, or sometimes their pasture contains a tick-infested dead tree. Ticks will almost invariably be found in the mane or tail of a pony and should be treated with a solution of regular tick dip for sheep or the like. When you see your pony trying to scratch his mane or tail, check for a tick or two. They suck blood and can swell up to the size of a marble. Usually, when this happens, there are two present—the big swollen one and a small one right underneath it.

If you're out riding and your pony steps on a bee's nest or a yellow jacket's nest, you may be in for trouble. Ride out of the area as quickly as possible. If your pony is stung, he will become terrified and bolt off in a mad gallop. More important, several stings can be a serious matter. For this you should keep some picric acid on hand in your first aid kit and apply some of the ointment to each sting, identifiable by the swollen knot around it. If you are near home and have ice cubes, apply them, although you may run out of hands and cold fingers before you're through. If you're out on the trail and have nothing for either yourself or your pony, apply cold mud liberally to the stung area and get yourself to a doctor as quickly as possible.

Worms

Ponies are contaminated by several different types of worms which sap their strength, dull their coat, and give them a listless look. Not only are worms dangerous, but they eat up a lot of valuable food in one form or another. You can never condition a wormy pony, and he will never have much stamina. Almost all ponies have worms to some degree, so many pony people worm their stock every six months. But such indiscriminate worming is not advisable because most vermifuges border on or are outright poisons by necessity. It's much better to take a sample of the pony's stool to a veterinarian and have him check it, then worm for whatever type is found to be present. Foals are especially prone to worms and should be checked at two months of age and again after weaning. Every pasture pony brought into the stable to condition for the show ring or racing competition should also be checked and wormed as necessary.

The principal worms you will find in ponies are:

1. Strongyels or bloodworms. About two inches and red in color, these are the most dangerous. They attach themselves to the intestinal tract and can work their way into the blood stream. If they happen to clog blood vessels it can lead to colic and sometimes death.

2. Ascarids or roundworms. These pencil-size white or gray worms are more trouble in foals than in older ponies. They consume a lot of the pony's intake of food, often make him pot-bellied and dull his coat and eyes.

3. Botfly larva. These are taken into the pony's mouth when he rubs off the little yellow eggs that botflies lay on his legs, flanks, and shoulders while at pasture. Once in the stomach, these eggs attach themselves to the wall where they grow into ugly red corrugated larva half to one inch long, damage the stomach lining, and cut down on the pony's ability to absorb food.

4. Pinworms. These are more a nuisance than serious. Straight and pin-like in size, they frequent the intestine near the anus and cause itching which may show up in rubbing of tails.

There are several compounds on the market which you can use to reduce drastically, if not eliminate, these worm problems. Some are powders and pills which must be administered orally; others you simply place in the food. If you want to be safe and sure, have your veterinarian check your pony and administer the proper remedy himself.

Your Vet

A pony is a tough and durable animal but when something goes wrong with him internally or externally, which won't be often, you must know a veterinarian to call for help. Often it may be an emergency or near emergency, so make the acquaintance of a good vet as soon as you buy your pony. Ask a local riding school or stable for the name of one. This way you'll be certain he specializes in equine medicine.

A veterinarian will be glad to go over the important protective measures your pony will need to keep in the pink of health. Sometimes, instead of making a personal call to your stable, he may be able to prescribe a simple remedy for your pony over the phone. Horse veterinarians are busy men and have to cover a lot of miles.

First Aid Kit

For the ordinary upkeep of your pony you will need a first aid kit, the contents of which your vet will be glad to list. There are first aid kits for horses and ponies which you can buy already made up, or you can put your own together. Keep it in a small suitcase or the like so you can carry it along to a show or trotting meet. All large shows have a vet on the premises for emergencies, but often you need only some minor thing from your first aid kit. It should contain the following:

1. A couple of big 12-inch rolls of cotton.
2. Set of leg raps for bandaging either for an injury or when transporting your pony.
3. Bottle of aspirin, 60 grain.
4. Bottle of white liniment or the like, for muscle soreness and bruises.
5. A colic remedy, either a preparation or baking soda.
6. A drench bottle for administering liquids.
7. A balling gun for administering tablets.
8. An antiseptic spray bomb for cuts, rope burns, saddle sores, and lesions.
9. Big jar of Vaseline.
10. Picric acid ointment for stings and burns.
11. Baking soda for muscular distention or colic.
12. Epsom salts for a laxative.
13. A twitch.
14. Scissors or knife.
15. A bar of castile soap and a soft sponge.

Illnesses

Books have been written on illnesses of horses and ponies. We can only touch here on those which you can positively identify and treat easily yourself. If you are not sure, don't take a chance. Call your vet and have him come for a checkup.

Cuts and Bruises—can be serious depending upon where they are located. A cut over the cannon from a kick can be much more difficult to heal than a large ugly-looking gash in the shoulder. If it is more than a nick, call your vet. Otherwise, wash it out clean with castile soap and spray with an antiseptic. A bruise in a muscle or tendon may be treated by rubbing the area with linament.

Coughs and Mild Colds—come in a wide variety of forms and can be symptomatic of other things, which is why no cough medicine was included in the first aid kit. Best thing is to put a blanket on your pony to keep him warm, feed him hot food like boiled oats with a little linseed mash, and call your vet. There is a good vaccine for influenza now, worth using if cases arise in your area.

Colic—amounts to a severe stomach-ache. A pony has a small sensitive stomach, and when he gorges on anything different from his usual diet —apples, too much grass in early spring—he will develop colic. Symptoms: groaning, rolling in discomfort, poking his sides with his muzzle. Treatment: don't let him lie down. Keep him on his feet, walk him, and call your vet immediately. He may prescribe the colic remedy in your first aid kit. But don't wait. Act quickly. Keep all water and food away from the pony until he shows definite improvement.

Encephalomyelitis or Sleeping Sickness—is a disease spread by mosquitoes and can be as harmful to ponies as to human beings. There is a protective two-shot injection with annual booster which is certainly worth using.

Shipping Fever—is a malady which comes from transporting ponies long distances. It only affects certain ponies, hence is thought to be similar to seasickness and possibly the result of irregularity of food and water and the interruption of normal physical relief during long trailer hauls. Symptoms are a sickly-looking pony with a temperature and no desire to eat or perform, which can be disastrous if you have paid to have him transported to a distant show or trail ride. Veterinary aid can be helpful before and after the ride.

Eye Infections—if they are minor, can be helped by bathing with a warm boric acid solution or using any good opthalmic preparation. However, runny eyes are more likely a symptom of something else. If they persist, have your pony checked.

Skin Punctures—are often deep and easily infected. Clean them out well, apply antiseptic and have vet give a shot of tetanus as a preventative against lockjaw. Same with a rusty nail in the foot.

Sprains—are the tearing of the ligaments around a joint when a pony steps in a hole or the like. The pony will be lame, and usually swelling will reveal the spot. Otherwise you'll have to track it down by checking his hoof, bending his fetlock, then his knee. If it's in his shoulder, stretch the leg to the front and up. He'll flinch when it hurts. If the sprain is low, stand your pony in a tub of cold water or in a cool stream. When the sprain is at the knee or above, wrap it with towels and apply hot water with epsom salts in it. Rest is imperative. Confine the pony to his stall and be sure to cut down on his feed while he's laid up.

Strains—are the result of pulling muscles or tendons. The affected area should be rubbed down with white liniment or other patent preparation which brings the blood to the area and helps in the healing. Rest is important, and again, cut down on his feed while he's laid up. If your pony develops a spavin or splint, it may require blistering, but this is a job for a vet.

Founder—or laminitis is the swelling of the flesh and blood vessels within the hard shell of the hoof. It is as though you had on a pair of boots and your feet suddenly swelled up twice their normal size and you tried to hobble around. This is how the pony feels. It comes from riding a pony too fast without warming him up first, riding him on a hard surface or working him to the point of exhaustion. Also, it can come from his gorging on too much grain, or being overfed and not exercised, or letting him stand still in a cold draft when he's hot. That's why it's important to walk your pony until he has cooled off. The moment you suspect your pony has founder, call your vet. Time is important. If you can't reach him, stand your pony in cool water or mud, but keep a blanket over him. A pony may be rendered permanently useless by founder, and there will always be white rings on his hoofs even if he recovers.

Diarrhea—is best brought under control by use of kaopectate. If this doesn't stop it, have your vet check further.

A Few Suggestions

Don't feed your pony too many tidbits. Lump sugar, apples, carrots are not harmful, but if you get him into the habit of expecting something every time you walk up to him, he'll begin to nip when he doesn't receive it. Nipping is not a trait of ponies. It is developed and should be stopped right in the beginning with a good slap on the nose every time your pony gives an indication of so doing.

All bad habits in ponies are either man-made or man-allowed. Don't let your pony get away with some little trick like brushing up against a tree when you're riding, or stopping to nibble a nice clump of grass. Soon these will become bad habits and you'll be angry at your pony for something that you allowed. If your pony kicks at others while out riding, cut yourself a snappy four-foot switch and sting his rear legs good and proper when he tries it. A couple of times of this will cure him of a dangerous prank.

Don't feed your pony lawn mower clippings. They sour quickly and can give him colic in short order.

After your pony has spent the winter in a stall, don't turn him loose in nice lush spring grass to eat to his heart's content. Colic will be the result. Change his diet slowly—an hour a day for a week, then two hours, then half a day, and so on.

If your pony starts to "weaving" in his stall, shifting his weight from side to side, it is a nervous habit resulting from the boredom of being confined. *Exercise him.* Let him run a little. Give him some freedom if you can't work him.

Boredom can lead to all kinds of bad habits. Chewing wood is one of them. Cribbing is another. In this habit the pony seizes a projecting surface between his teeth, stretches his neck and audibly sucks in air. A confirmed cribber is difficult, if not impossible, to cure, and the consequences internally can be serious. Cribbing straps and muzzles help, but when you cease using them the pony returns to his old act. The best cure is *work* and *exercise.*

Another little trick is catching your pony in the pasture when you want to ride him. This isn't always as simple as it sounds. There are two ways: luring him, and force training him to come when called. You lure him with a metal quart measure which has a handful of oats and a couple of stones the size of a golf ball in it. Rattling this and rewarding him with the oats soon gets him to coming on the run when he hears the signal—but it doesn't always work. He may not be hungry, or he may get wise that the rattle also means he's going for a ride. Thus the force training system is better but should be done by an adult.

You start off in a box stall with the pony. Have a buggy whip or long switch in your right hand. Extend your left hand and say, "Come, Peter, Come!" Use your pony's name and repeat it rhythmically, "Come, Skip, Come!" The pony won't know what you mean, so you tap him on the rump with the switch. He will scoot along the wall and into your extended hand, at which point you pet him fondly, step to the other side of the stall and repeat. Soon he learns that he'd better come when you give that rhythmic call. The next test is outside in a small area like one corner of his paddock. Use the same procedure and repeat it until he comes immediately. When he gets a little balky, corner him and give him a sharp rap on the rump. If you have any trouble outside, put a rope on him at first so he can't get away. Let him be twenty or thirty feet away, make your rhythmic call and give him a good jerk on the rope until he comes. Once he's trained to come when called in the paddock, try the pasture. You shouldn't have any trouble.

One word of caution, in all your training, be serious about it, and never deceive him.

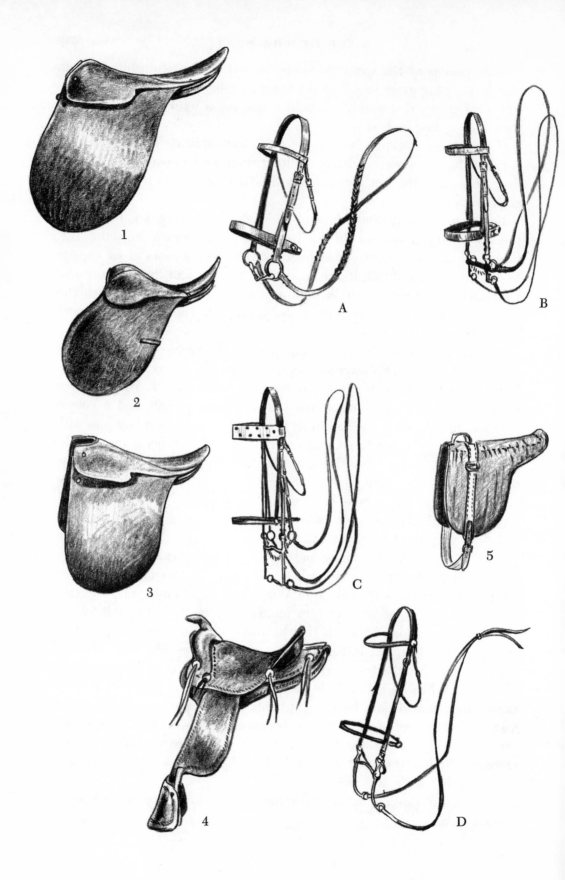

1

2

3

4

A

B

C

5

D

Tack and harness

Tack refers to bridles and saddles used in riding a pony. Harness applies to the driving equipment put on a pony to pull a roadster, viceroy, chariot, wagon, and the like.

If your pony is broken to ride when you buy him, be sure to ask what kind of bridle is used on him. You may even be able to buy all his tack—bridle, saddle, and halter—right along with him. In this way you will be sure it fits and that the pony is used to it.

Each type of pony wears a different kind of bridle and saddle. That is, a jumping pony will have a different saddle, bridle, and bit than a Tennessee Walking pony. The principal tack and its purposes are illustrated here, also the proper way to hold the reins.

For regular fun riding the best outfit is either the English saddle with plain snaffle bridle or the Western saddle with Western bridle which has the same jointed snaffle bit. The other types of bridles and saddles are for more advanced and competitive riding of various styles. Bits are important too, for they are what persuades the pony to mind you when you're riding him. As the pony becomes older, its mouth often becomes tougher and less sensitive to reining. To correct this, a different type of bit can be resorted to, but it is best to consult an experienced horseman in this.

Driving bridles are constructed a little differently than riding bridles. They have long reins which are properly called lines, and blinders which prevent the pony from becoming frightened as something passes it. The lines on trotting ponies have loops in them called hand holds. In this way the driver has immediate and powerful control of his pony.

There are several different types of pony driving harness, depending upon whether the vehicle to be drawn is a viceroy, sulky, carriage, coach, gig, governess cart, or what. Single harness is different from double harness for a pair of ponies. Tandem and multi-hitches are different too. Basically, it all works on the same principle. When a pony pulls forward, the stress of the vehicle's weight is on his shoulders; when he stops, something must keep the vehicle from running into his rear end.

In single harness, the vehicle which the pony draws will be light, so a

Pony Tack: 1. English saddle for all-purpose riding; 2. jumping saddle with deep forward seat and knee rolls; 3. show saddle for Gaited and Walking ponies; 4. Western saddle for all-purpose, Western-style riding; 5. bareback pad with hand hold for riding a pony comfortably and safely without a saddle. A) pony snaffle bridle with laced rein, used with saddles 1. and 2. for general riding, hunting and jumping; B) English pelham bridle with pelham bit and double reins, also used with saddles 1. and 2. for greater control of the pony; C) show bridle with curb and snaffle bits and curbchain, used with saddle 3. for showing Three- and Five-Gaited ponies; D) Western bridle with aluminum Western bit for use with saddle 4.

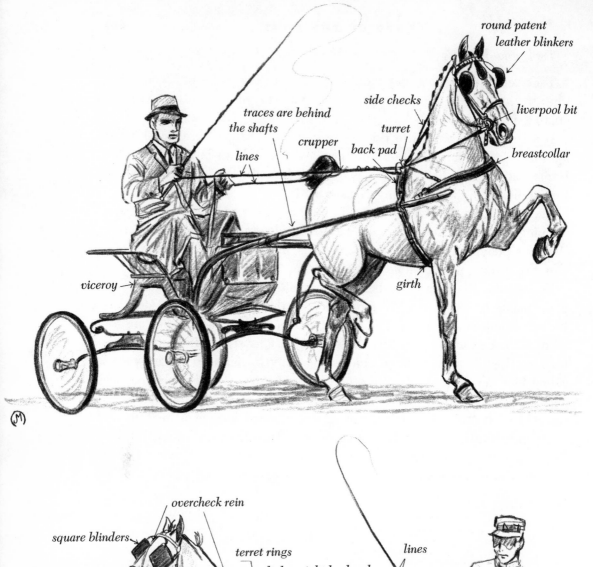

round patent
leather blinkers

side checks

liverpool bit

traces are behind
the shafts

turret

crupper

back pad

breastcollar

lines

viceroy

girth

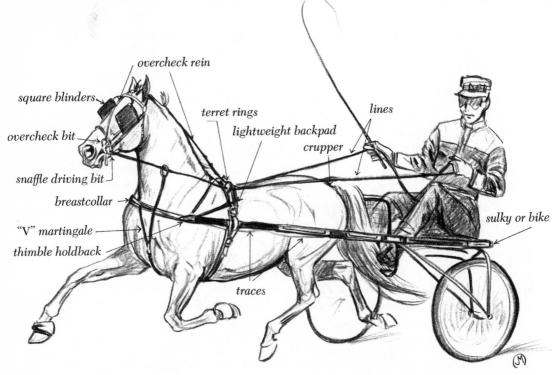

overcheck rein

square blinders

terret rings

lines

overcheck bit

lightweight backpad

crupper

snaffle driving bit

breastcollar

sulky or bike

"V" martingale

thimble holdback

traces

Opposite top: Fine harness of the show pony.
Opposite bottom: Racing harness for trotting and roadster ponies.
Below: Heavy duty pony driving harness.

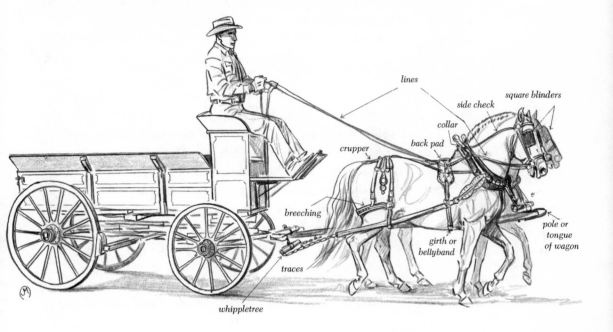

breast strap across the chest is enough to pull it. This type of harness is
lighter in weight for the racing pony and more refined and flashy for
the show pony. In this latter instance, fine harness means more delicate
and beautifully made, which is why show pony harness is always trimmed
with patent leather.

In fine harness pairs, the ponies wear hames which are light patent
leather collars to which the traces are attached, and there is a pole between the ponies instead of shaves as a single pony uses.

Heavy harness with stout shoulder collars, chunky traces, and breeching is used when the pony team has a real pulling job to do like a wagon,
stagecoach, or heavy weight in pony pulling contests.

Pony harness consists basically of the following:

1. *Bridle* and *lines.*
2. *Breast collar* or *hames* or *heavy collar.*
3. *Saddle* – is a narrow pad over the back, held in place by a girth. On
   its top are rings or terrets through which the lines pass; on its sides
   are leather loops which hold the shafts.

4. *Traces* – are long leather straps running from the breast collar to the singletree and take the strain of the pulling.

5. *Checkrein* or *overhead check* – is a strap running from the crown or top of the bridle down the crest of the pony and attaching to the saddle. Its purpose is to keep his head up.

6. *Crupper* – is a strap running from the saddle down the pony's back and under his tail. It acts as a balance to the checkrein to keep the saddle in place.

7. *Breeching* – is a wide horizontal strap passing around the lower part of the pony's rump. It keeps the vehicle from running into the pony's back end when he stops or goes downhill. High-stepping fine harness ponies do not use breeching. The shafts are slipped through the leather loops in the saddle and tied down by a strap.

8. *Thimbles* – are little cups which go over the ends of the shafts of sulkies and roadsters, and are connected by straps to the saddle. Thimbles are used to stop these light carts instead of heavy breeching which might encumber the stride and speed of a racing pony.

Stallion tack is often used to show mature ponies in in-hand events where they are expected to exhibit the ultimate in class and way of going.

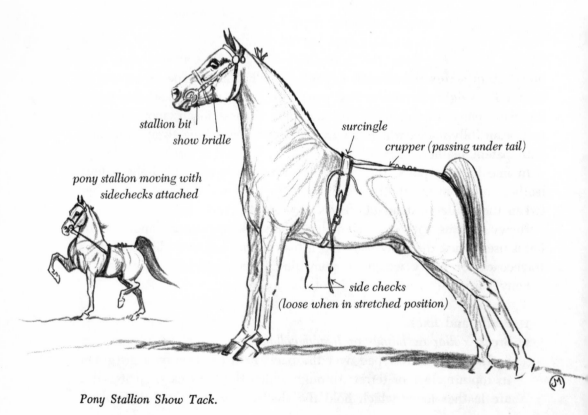

stallion bit
show bridle

surcingle

crupper (passing under tail)

pony stallion moving with
sidechecks attached

side checks
(loose when in stretched position)

Pony Stallion Show Tack.

This tack includes a show bridle and harness saddle with side checks which make the pony arch his neck and keep him better collected.

In a model class where the pony is judged on conformation alone, he must be shown in a bridle only. Some exhibitors use the pony stallion show lead bridle with horseshoe-patterned bit-rings and a leather lead line. Others use a regular pony bridle with the reins as a lead.

Tack and harness are expensive, but with good care, the leather will provide many years of use. Develop the habit of cleaning off the bridle and saddle each time after use, also the harness and vehicle.

When you remove the saddle from your pony, wipe off the under side of it with a damp sponge and some saddle soap, also the girth. This will remove the sweat while it is still damp and fresh. If you let it cake on, you'll have a problem and the pony will be exceedingly uncomfortable under saddle.

When you remove the bridle, jounce the lower half in a pail of water to clean the bit. Wipe off any part which has gotten sweat-coated. This little bit of work now will have the tack ready for use the next time you ride.

Whenever your bridle and saddle get soaked in a rainstorm, don't put them near a heater or stove. Let them dry out naturally, then go over every inch of them with a good leather conditioner obtainable from any harness store. Be sure to cover the sharp bends at buckles and rings extra well. This is where cracking first begins. Saddle soap and a damp hot sponge have long been the horseman's favorite way of cleaning tack and harness, but several modern leather conditioners and restorers are on the market now. All require that you at least get around to using them.

Stirrups should be polished and bits kept clean. Washing the lower portion of the bridle in a pail of water as suggested above will get the horse's saliva and most of the foreign matter off the bit, but it should be polished occasionally to keep it sanitary and in top condition, especially if you store it.

Harness is cared for in the same way as good tack. In fact, fine show harness is among the most immaculately-kept equipment in the whole of the horse world. Every brass fitting is polished to a glitter and the patent leather gleams like black glass when the ponies come high-stepping into the ring.

To achieve this requires work. If the harness is soiled after use, it is gone over with a damp hot sponge to remove the dirt. The patent leather is kept as dry as possible. Patent leather cream is used to maintain its glistening surface. The rest of the harness is washed down and a top grade of black shoe polish used to cover up scratches.

The superbly fitted carriages, regardless of their size, are maintained

*Pony vehicles come in a variety of fascinating forms and sizes. A few shown here are:
1. viceroy or show buggy complete with patent leather fenders and dash, for the fine
harness pony; 2. old-fashioned surrey with the fringe on top, pony size, having black
canopy with red fringe and black seats trimmed with red leather; 3. pony buckboard
with spring-mounted seat and wooden dash; 4. pony slat cart for training and fun
driving; 5. pony trap cart for country driving and costume classes; 6. pony stage coach,
a replica of the famous Concord coach for 2–6 ponies; 7. Conestoga wagon, pony size,
a reproduction of the famous freight wagon that carried settlers westward; 8. racing
sulky; 9. governess cart with wicker basket sides and back door, corduroy upholstery,
hickory, coup-point shafts and rubber-tired wheels; 10. pony wagon, exact replica of the
old-fashioned farm wagon, complete with brake and shafts, pole or stiff tongue, for two-,
four-, and six-pony hitches.*

6

7

8

9

10

Jeanne
Mellin
'65

with equal care. Viceroys, after coming from the show ring, are washed down with a mild soap and water. Any chips in the sparkling enamel finish are touched up, and twice a year the vehicle is waxed with a high gloss floor or furniture wax. The vehicle is stored in fleece-lined canvas covers fitted to enclose the wheels, body, shafts, and pole.

A sulky or cart should be wiped off with a damp cloth or sponge each time after use, especially if the track has been muddy. The fittings should be carefully maintained and once a year the whole vehicle should be given a coat of spar varnish to cover nicks and scrapes and preserve the hardwood shafts. The chrome wheels should be kept polished and the bearings well lubricated. Most sulkies fold up for easy transportation and storage. They are best stored vertically in a tack room so the shafts lean up against a wall. Nothing can step on or run over the shafts then, and they will keep their camber. Around the track, a sulky should always be stood up when not in use.

Daily working harness for show ponies and trotters should be cleaned with a sponge and warm water and saddle soap or other leather preserver the same as regular riding tack. The rubber bell boots and scalpers should be washed free of mud and grime, and whatever ankle or knee boots the pony may wear should be wiped off or brushed. If you don't attend to these little details, your pony may develop chafe sores that will be hard to heal.

Every once in a while you will come across an old saddle or harness set in a dusty barn or at an auction. The leather will be dried out, but if it isn't cracked and you can buy it cheaply, you may be able to restore it to something worthwhile. Saddles restore much better than bridles or harness for the simple reason that there aren't so many bends. If the leather is badly cracked or broken, your efforts will be a waste of time. Once the leather goes dead and dries out in a harness or bridle, it is hardly safe to use again. If you want to try to restore a saddle, use a liquid leather conditioner that penetrates deeply, not a soap or a wax. Work slowly. Cover every bit of the leather. Give it at least three treatments before you try to use it. You can tell by the feel whether the leather has regained its life or not. Be sure it's safe before you try to use it.

Chapter 19

Training Your Pony

There are two basic areas in which to train your pony—riding and driving. A fun pony you need only teach to be ridden. A competition pony must afterward be trained as a jumper, Western using, parade or other saddle type of pony. If you want a chariot, trotting, roadster, or any other harness type of pony, you will first have to teach him to drive, then develop him as a specialist later. Teaching your pony is a matter of time, patience, and persistence. It isn't difficult because he has intelligence. You may not think so at first but this is where your patience and persistence come into play.

Let's start off with the riding area of training. Naturally, you must know how to ride before you can teach your pony how to be ridden. This is another way of saying that your first pony should be completely trained so you can learn from him. After you gain experience and knowledge, you can train one for yourself. To be sure you know the proper ways to bridle and saddle your pony, mount, dismount, and so forth, we'll run through them here.

A basic rule is that your pony's bridle and saddle must fit properly. If the bridle is too tight, the pony will be in pain; too loose, it will not allow you to control him, and may even fall off his head. If the saddle is too loose, it can turn right under the pony when you try to mount, or it may give him back sores from the loose rubbing.

When you put the tack on the pony for a ride, the bridle always goes on first. Stand on the near or left side of the pony facing his head. Slip the reins over his head and neck so you have a little control over him when you take off his halter. With the crown of the bridle in your right hand and the bit in your left, slip his muzzle into the cavesson, the bit into his mouth, and work the crown over his ears and into place. Make sure nothing is twisted, then buckle the throatlatch slackly. The bit should ride just at the corners of the pony's mouth. If it sags below that, tighten up on the cheek straps evenly; if it pulls up enough to wrinkle the corners of the mouth, let the cheek straps out a bit.

Don't tie your pony by the reins while you get the saddle or any other

Opposite:

Learn to mount your pony properly. It is always done from the left or near side. Stand by the pony's left shoulder, the reins gathered in your left hand tight enough so there's no slack. Toss the bight or loose rein loop over to the opposite side, out of the way, and take hold of the saddle's pommel or a handful of the pony's mane with your left hand. Raise your left foot and place it securely in the stirrup with the right hand as shown in the first illustration. Immediately place your right hand on the cantle or back of the saddle, give a skip and a jump with your right foot, pull with both hands and you're up. Don't pause in this position, but swing your right leg over the pony's rump as shown in the second illustration. Settle down into the saddle and slip your foot into the stirrup first thing. Hold the reins as shown in the third illustration, and you're ready to go. Dismounting is merely the reverse of this. Practice both until you have the timing down perfectly. In the beginning, have someone hold the pony's head just to be on the safe side.

time, or you'll be forever breaking reins. If he won't stand patiently and wait, snap a cross-tie into a bit ring.

The saddle is placed on the pony from the near side. If it is a Western saddle, a blanket is first placed on the back and smoothed off. A pad can be, but is seldom, used with an English saddle. Work the saddle on the pony's back so it rests naturally and well forward. Fasten the girth up tight enough so you can just about wedge your fingers under it but not slide them around loosely. A wise old pony will hold his breath while you tighten, so you may have to lead him ten or twelve feet and tighten again when the air is out of him.

Check the stirrups for approximately the correct length by holding them up to your arm. They should come snugly under your armpit when your arm and fingers are extended to the stirrup catch on the saddle.

To mount, stand on the left side of your pony, facing the saddle, reins gathered up in your left hand, which has hold of the pommel of the saddle. Use your right hand to hold the stirrup while you put your left toe into it. Then place your right hand on the cantle of the saddle, give a bounce with your right leg, pull yourself up with your arms, and swing your right leg over the pony's rump and settle down into the saddle. Immediately get your foot into the other stirrup for safety. Then you are ready to go.

Remember: You don't take off at a gallop. You walk your pony several minutes first to warm up his body and get the circulation moving through his feet. Then you trot him awhile. At the end of your ride you reverse this procedure and walk him ten minutes to cool him off and slow down his circulation.

Bridle chafing occurs when the bridle doesn't fit properly or is in a dirty condition. Chafe spots form into sores, particularly around the ears, poll, and temples. Adjust your bridle as previously described, put some Vaseline on the chafe spots and let them heal before you continue riding. Sometimes corners of the lip are painfully pinched by the joint where the ring joins the mouth piece.

In case your bridle breaks you can do right well using a snug halter temporarily in its place. Two small double-end snaps attached to the side rings of the halter will hold the bit in place; and for reins you can snap two lead ropes right into the rings of the bit. Remember that the halter must fit quite snugly to the pony's head to begin with because the only adjustment you have is in how much you tighten the headstrap. But I've seen public stables and even veteran riders use this rig on the trial because it's so handy. To take the bit out of the mouth temporarily you simply unsnap one side, slip the bit out of the pony's mouth, fold it around to the other side of the halter and snap it to the upper ring which holds

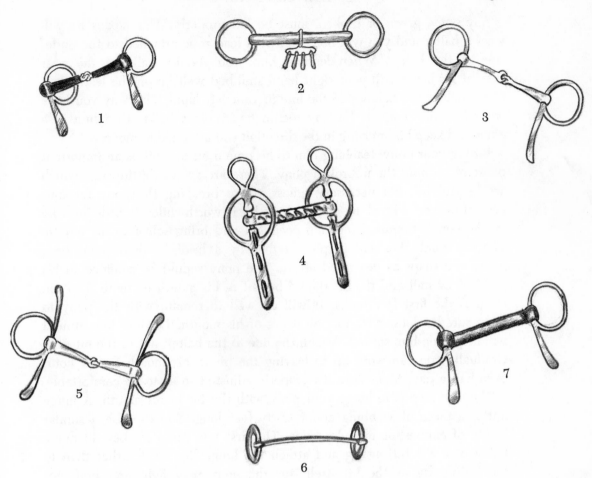

Driving bits come in a variety of forms: 1. is rubber mouth snaffle half cheek, used for soft-mouthed ponies; 2. is mouthing bit with tongue lugs which keep saliva in pony's mouth; 3. is snaffle half cheek, the most common all-purpose driving bit; 4. is Liverpool bit, used on most all fine harness ponies, has four possible positions for the lines— inside the circle, the top slot which is called the "half cheek" position, the middle slot which is called the "first curb," and the lower slot, called the "second curb" and used on ponies that are pullers; 5. is a snaffle full cheek, used mostly as a training bit for ponies that "yaw" (open their mouths too much; the full cheeks prevent the bit from slipping through the pony's mouth when open); 6. is an overcheck bit, used with an overcheck line to keep the pony's head high; 7. is rubber chain half cheek, for roadster and racing ponies and training young colts to the bit.

the bit against the pony's cheek and allows him to graze or relax while you eat lunch or the like. Or the bit can be entirely removed by unsnapping both snaps. This rig should not be used on a green pony, but on a gentle old-timer it works fine.

Any pony, green or broken, must be led properly. This means he will wear a halter and you will hold him by a lead rope attached to the under side of the halter. When leading him, you should walk on the near side, at his head with your right hand snubbed well up on the lead, close to the halter, the balance of the line in your left hand. This way you have control of the pony. If for any reason he becomes balky, turn him in a circle and keep him moving in the direction you intended to move.

Bitting your pony, teaching him to become used to a bit, is an important phase of training the unbroken pony. There are special bitting rigs which are helpful but not necessary unless you're breaking the pony for harness. However, a breaking or mouthing bit is worthwhile; its little keys lie on the pony's tongue, keep him occupied and bring saliva to his mouth. The bit should be held in place either by a bridle without reins or a halter and snaps as described above. The pony should be confined to his paddock or stall and the bit should be left in his mouth no more than ten minutes the first few times. It will do well to remain with the pony to make sure he doesn't try to paw it out of his mouth. Leading him around will help keep him settled. Attach the line to the halter, not to the bit ring. Gradually you can work up to leaving the bit in his mouth for an hour, even half a day. Make sure it's properly adjusted so as to be comfortable.

The next step is to lunge your pony with the bit in his mouth. A lunge line is a piece of webbing about thirty feet long. You can use a similar length of clothesline or nylon rope. The first few times it's best to put a halter over the bitting rig and attach the lunge line to it rather than to the bitting rig or the bit itself, for the pony may fight and pull, not knowing quite what to do. The idea is to have the pony go around you in a circle at various speeds and gaits. It is excellent exercise and you can teach your pony a great deal, especially verbal commands like "Whoa!" and "Walk!" and "Trot!" Keep the sessions brief—ten or fifteen minutes. Work the pony clockwise half the time and counterclockwise half the time.

If at first you have trouble getting your pony to go around you in a circle, run ahead of him fifteen or twenty feet fast enough to break him into a trot, then step off to the side and keep him going. He'll soon get the knack of it and love the workout. He can be walked, trotted, and cantered, all on a lunge line, and remember that he must be warmed up slowly and cooled off afterward. There are lunging whips which you may or may not want to use.

At this point you can introduce the pony to the saddle. Let him smell and see it, and have someone hold him or fasten him to cross-ties while you slip the saddle over his rump and settle it into place. You won't do more than rest it on his back the first couple of times. Then walk him

Lunging your pony is important for exercising and training. A bitting rig, as shown here, is fine training for the green pony but a regular halter will serve just as well for the mature pony. When lunging your pony with a bit it is best to run the lunge line through the bit ring, over the top of the pony's head and down the other side, snapping it to the bit ring on the side farthest from you. That keeps an even tension on the bit. Walk the pony first to warm up his legs, then trot him, always in a circle around you. Slap the ground behind him with the whip to keep him moving. After a while, reverse him and work him in the other direction. If your pony has not had much exercise, ten or fifteen minutes of lunging before taking him out to ride may keep him from cutting up or even bucking you off.

around with the saddle very lightly cinched. As the pony becomes accustomed to this thing on his back, tighten the cinch so the saddle can't slide about, then take him out and lunge him through a walk and trot with it on his back. Remove the stirrups the first couple of times so they won't dangle around and slap against his sides and frighten him. Soon you'll be able to cinch the saddle up tight and put him through all his paces on the lunge with the stirrups bouncing merrily.

You are now ready to mount your pony. He should be two years or older so his back will have developed sufficiently to take your weight. Of course, each day as you tack up your pony to lunge him, you put your arm in the stirrup and bear down on it a little so he becomes used to weight being applied to him. Carry this a little further; have someone hold the pony's head while you step in the stirrup, stand up and lay your weight across the saddle two or three times. Throw half a bag of grain over the saddle and lead him around. Finally the day comes when your friend holds the pony's head and you stand up in the stirrup, swing your right leg over his rump and settle into the saddle.

Because the pony accepts you calmly in the beginning doesn't mean that one day he won't suddenly decide he doesn't want you on his back any longer, duck his head, arch his back and give a good snappy bounce trying to toss you off. Be prepared. If you can keep his head up, he won't be very successful.

The first few times you ride your pony, have your friend lead him slowly and carefully so you can let the reins lie slackly on his neck. When you want to make a left turn, your friend will pull the left rein gently but positively and lead the pony in that direction. Same for a right turn. This way the pony learns what the pull on the particular rein means and at the same time he is under complete control. After two or three days of this, you can mount him and ride him under your own guidance within the ring or paddock. You'll have to exaggerate the rein directions at first, but in a short while he'll catch on. If you wish to teach your pony to neck rein, cross the reins under his neck. Thus when you bend the reins against one side of his neck, he will feel a pull in the other direction and go that way.

Walk the pony for the first week. Practice getting on and off and having him stand still while you're doing this. If you have taught him the command "Whoa!" it will be easy.

After you and your pony are doing well at a walk, you can ease him into a trot and begin to post up and down to the rhythm of his stride. Practice this a couple of weeks, shifting every little distance from a walk to a trot back to a walk again. Then one day when your pony is well warmed up, ease him into a canter. This does not mean a fast gallop but rather a gentle canter just slightly faster than a trot. Make haste slowly in all your training and when your pony doesn't master a certain stage, stick with him patiently until he accomplishes it before you advance to the next step.

It's important that you teach your pony to back. Don't saw on his mouth and expect him to do it. Have someone stand in front of him while you are mounted. Let him take hold of the reins close to the bit and gently force the pony backward while you say "Back! Back!" If the pony is confused and doesn't understand, get a light switch and have your friend tap him

Champion Parade Pony, Stardust, with his thirteen-year-old owner-rider, Danny Swartz of Durant, Iowa, has won the Parade Stake Championship at the Iowa State Fair '63 and '64, Shrine Show Parade Stake at Cedar Rapids, Iowa, '63 and '64, and the World's Champion Parade Pony stake at the American Royal Show, Kansas City, Missouri, '63 and '64. Note the superb action of this 53-inch red roan mare, the brilliant parade trappings, and Danny's perfect riding form.

lightly on the knees as he repeats the process. A pony's knees are very sensitive and he will back promptly though you must practice in order to have him do it smoothly.

Here are some training tips:

Treat your pony's mouth gently. Don't saw on it or jerk the reins unless the pony is misbehaving. The more responsive you are through the reins and bit, the better he will perform.

Best place to train is in a ring or your paddock. The pony can't run away with you. If he ever starts to run away, lean back in the saddle and pull hard on one rein so he has to run in a circle.

A pony can only buck with his head lowered. If your pony tries this, get his head up with a couple of quick jerks on the reins. A pony that is overfed and underexercised will almost invariably buck a couple of times when you first start out for a ride. Sometimes he may buck if the equipment isn't adjusted properly. The girth may be twisted, something else pinching or tickling him.

It's always a good idea to lunge your pony ten minutes or let him run in the paddock for half an hour before you start to train him. This will get the devil out of his system and make him more receptive to your instruction.

Rearing is when the pony stands on his hind legs. If he is not being ridden, chances are it's only a playful gesture, but it's one that should not be cultivated. Picking small foals up by their front feet to pet them like dogs can start it. If your pony rears when you're riding him, lean forward and throw your weight against his neck or give him a good crack with your hand between the ears. Often, your pony may rear if he is suddenly frightened. This is his way of self-preservation, and he thinks only of striking out with his front feet at the danger facing him. If your pony is a confirmed rearer, get rid of him or have a professional horseman break him of this dangerous habit. He can go over backward and if you're not nimble enough to slide off to the side you can be seriously hurt.

Shying is a sign of fright wherein the pony takes a sudden side step or throws his head up. It's usually the overfed and underworked, spirited pony that does this, but you should dismount and lead your pony over to the object that caused him to shy, often a shadow or a bright tin can. Also, you should accustom your pony to noises of all kinds, traffic and other distractions, particularly if you plan to show him or ride him in a parade. Ponies have good steady temperaments and will do whatever they are used to doing or have been trained to do.

You should also teach your pony to enter a trailer, or the day will come when you want to take him to a show and he won't load. If you have a two-pony trailer that hitches to the back of a car, the best way to train your pony to enter it easily is to park it right in the paddock and feed him in it. In a couple of days he'll consider it his second stall. Before you haul him off to a show, pull him around the block so he gets used to the actual motion of riding in the trailer.

If you buy a pony at an auction that won't load, run a good long rope from the pony's halter to the front of the trailer around a support, then all the way back and behind the pony's rump. This way, when you inch the pony forward, the slack is taken up front and back. With a little help you can soon work him into the trailer. Having a ramp always helps. Many ponies don't like to step up and into a narrow, dark enclosure.

Your riding pony is now well trained and a pleasure to ride. You can continue to advance his training and make him into a jumper, parade pony, Western using pony or gymkhana expert.

Your pony should be at least three years old before you begin teaching him to jump. His bones, joints, tendons, and ligaments must be hard and strong enough to take the strain.

Most ponies jump well for their size but tend to "bunny-hop" over their fences rather than stand back and take them in stride. They have to be trained not to get too close to an obstacle and jump straight up with a hollow back and high head, but rather to take it with a striding ease, head lowered and back rounded.

Two other major objectives are to teach your pony to jump calmly as though enjoying it, and never to run out around or to refuse a fence. Again, make haste slowly. Jumping makes heavy demands on a pony's strength and muscles as well as his brain. Ten or fifteen minutes a day is plenty. And always remember, five minutes every day is far better than half an hour once a week. Conditioning is important, for your pony will be using and developing different muscles.

Using cavalettis or wooden poles to train the jumping pony.

To start, place six jumping bars (octagonal 5-inch poles 12 feet long and preferably painted white) on the ground in a straight line about five feet apart for ponies up to 48 inches, six feet apart for ponies up to 52 inches and seven to eight feet apart for large ponies. The first couple of times, lead your pony at a walk over these white obstacles. Let him sniff

To have a good jumping pony you must train not only the pony but also yourself until you become a well-coordinated team. Practice on low jumps, over and over, until you know your mount. Practice over different types of jumps and at different times of the day so he sees them under different lighting conditions. Let the height come later. Here youthful Linda Donaldson takes Liseter Blue Mist over a practice hurdle with perfect jumping style. Confidence of pony and rider is evident.

them, look at them, and grow accustomed to them. Then mount up and trot him over them several times. They should be spaced so they are a shade more than a stride apart. This way he will have to stretch out a bit.

Each time your pony crosses a bar, you should practice the proper way to jump. Train yourself to look at an imaginary point twenty to thirty feet ahead and at the same time move your hands halfway up the pony's crest and shift your weight forward just slightly onto your hands. This releases the reins so the pony can extend his head and jump. Remember the lowered head and rounded back. The pony can't achieve this if you don't let up on the reins as he leaves the ground, and never jerk on him at this point. Also, you never jump in a Western saddle, always in a forward-seat, jumping saddle with a knee roll.

When the pony becomes proficient at trotting over the poles and you have the habit of moving your hands to his crest, leaning forward and then straightening up as you pass over each one, you're ready for your first jump. Increase the distance between the last two poles about two feet and put a bushel basket upside down under one end of the last pole. This will raise one side of it about a foot off the ground. Practice riding this a few times, then raise the other end of the pole to the same height. Maintain the same speed and direction, trot right down the center of the poles, and you can be pretty certain of getting your pony to jump the last one. If he does it properly, pet and congratulate him, then take him off for a pleasant ride.

In training your pony, always try to end with a job done correctly. Don't make him repeat something over and over until he makes a mistake and then stop for the day. If he does the first jump properly, let him remember it that way. If he doesn't, try another time or two but no more.

Soon your pony will be jumping like a veteran over one pole. Remember the importance of your part in the process. You must give him plenty of rein as he goes over the jump. He will enjoy jumping this way, whereas if you jerk on the reins as he springs, you may bring him down on top of the bar and so frighten him that he won't ever want to try again. The pony is so handy that he can get himself out of most any kind of trouble if his rider doesn't interfere.

After you and your pony have mastered the first jump, raise the other poles and have a series of six small jumps. This is great practice, but two or three times down the line is enough for a daily workout. Gradually you can vary the distances between the poles. Set up a pair 12 to 15 feet apart; move two close together only two feet apart so the pony stretches a little in going over them. Give him a stride between jumps, two strides between jumps, or just in and out. Don't make any higher than 14 to 18 inches.

Remember to keep your pony aimed straight down the middle of the row of jumps. Lean forward each time to give the pony plenty of rein. If you slip or get a little off balance, grab his mane and hold on, don't grab the saddle. Keep your weight on your heels. This will cushion your landing better. Keep your calfs snug against the saddle and your knees against the knee-roll. Give your pony a good leg squeeze or a kick as you come into each jump to urge him on. Soon you both will pick up the rhythm involved in jumping.

If your pony stands under 50 inches, don't jump him over two feet; or two feet six inches if he is a larger pony. Don't raise the bars until you're sure he will jump anything at a lower level. When you want your pony to jump a new type of obstacle, lead him up to it so he can look it over. And keep it low in height the first couple of times. Take in some shows to see the various types of jumps that can be set up. Where you go from here is up to you. It might be to Olympic or International Jumping someday.

To train the parade pony you must develop action. This means that his hoofs must grow long so he can be shod with weighted shoes. The parade pony generally has a lot of Saddlebred or Hackney blood in him. This gives him naturally high action.

The two required show gaits are the animated, graceful walk and a high-prancing trot called the parade gait. These gaits are best developed by a professional horseman to the stage where the young amateur can take over and show the pony. For showing the parade pony you need a fancy parade outfit which includes a beautiful saddle and bridle, and you as the rider must wear fancy Western or Mexican dress—cowboy suit, hat, boots, spurs.

The parade pony has to be well-mannered as well as princely-gaited. He is faulted for excessive speed, switching tail, exaggerated opening of mouth, lugging on the bridle and fighting the bit, halting or hesitating, zigzagging or sidewise movement, or for ears that are not alertly carried. Judging is 75 percent on performance, manners, and conformation of pony, and 25 percent on appointments of pony and rider.

The Western using pony is trained for roping, reining, cutting, and other Western competitive events. It is best to start with a pony no younger than three years old, even four, because he must be fairly mature and well broken to Western riding. In most cases you will need special facilities and equipment. Cutting and roping will require sheep or calves for practice. Some lightweight professional horsemen train ponies for Western competition, but you can do it yourself by carefully following regular Quarter Horse training procedures, and if the pony turns out well, you'll have a valuable animal.

POA Indian costume class shows contestants and mounts colorfully decorated. Three of the five ponies, ridden here with only a thong in the mouth, are mature stallions.

The mud flies as pony swings around the last barrel for home and rider takes quirk from between her teeth as a gentle reminder.

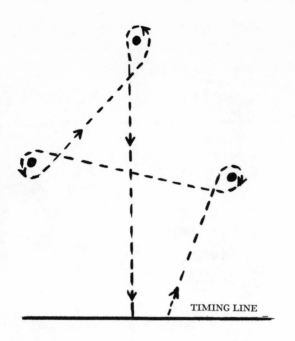

A.   CLOVER-LEAF BARREL RACE

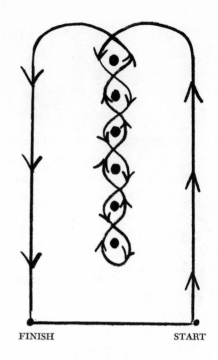

B.   BENDING RACE

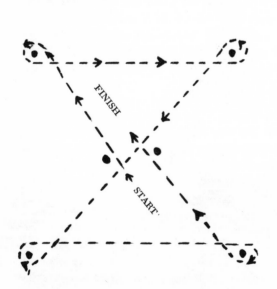

C.   QUADRANGLE STAKE RACE

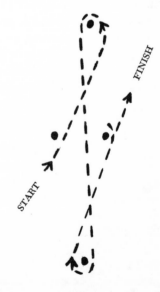

D.   FIGURE-EIGHT STAKE RACE

The Western riding pony can be used for pleasure riding in pony and horse show classes, trail riding and gymkhana events. To teach your pony barrel racing or pole bending, it is best to set up a series of barrels or poles at home and practice there.

Let's turn now to training the driving pony.

The first step is to see that he leads properly, and this will be particularly important if you want to show him in model classes as a yearling. This is the general procedure. It gives the pony experience around crowds and provides the basic training of alertness and poise so vital to the show pony. The pony is also taught to stretch and stand still.

Training for harness can begin for the two-year-old pony when the good

Opposite:

You and your pony can have great fun entering some of the events at pony shows, pony rallies, and Gymkhanas. These include, in addition to the four above, the Keyhole Race, Relay Race, Rescue Race, Novelty Race, Trailer Race, and Musical Chairs. If you have enough room at home, set up a barrel racing course or a string of poles, and train your pony to work them perfectly and with speed. Move at a trot in the beginning, then gradually increase the speed. In a short while, he'll get all fired up every time he sees a barrel or a line of poles. Remember always to limber him up well before you race him. The following are the rules for the four most popular events which are diagrammed above:

A—Barrel Race. This is a timed class with three barrels in a clover-leaf pattern as indicated in the drawing; 40 feet minimum distance between any two barrels, 20 feet minimum distance between any barrel and the timing line. Any variance from the running pattern means elimination. A five-second penalty for each barrel knocked down; no penalty for touching a barrel.

B—Pole Bending. In this timed class, six stakes are set 20 feet apart in a straight line down the center of the ring, first stake 20 feet from the timing line. Rider usually has his choice of which side to pass first stake, but from then on must continue in the same manner. A two-second penalty for knocking down a stake; if it interferes with the completion of the course, you're disqualified. No penalty for merely touching a stake.

C—Quadrangle Stake Race. In this timed event four stakes form a square 25 yards on each side. Two additional stakes are placed 5 yards apart in the center of the square for a start-and-finish line. A running start is permitted and the course must be patterned as indicated. Knocking down a stake or touching one with either hand by rider (some try to hold them up!) constitutes a two-second penalty which is added to total time.

D—Figure-Eight Stake Race. For this timed event two stakes are placed near opposite ends of the ring and two stakes 20 feet apart at center of the ring. Each entry takes a running start and must follow the pattern indicated in the diagram. A two-second penalty is applied for each stake knocked down, but none for touching one. Rounding both end stakes in the same direction shortens the course and thus disqualifies you.

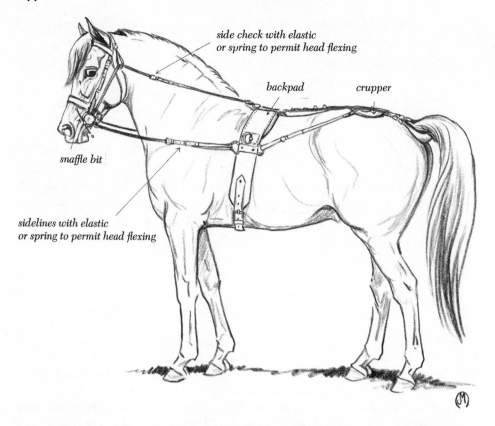

side check with elastic
or spring to permit head flexing

backpad   crupper

snaffle bit

sidelines with elastic
or spring to permit head flexing

Bitting harness for the pony. This completely adjustable rig is used to introduce the bit and reins to the green pony. Both sidechecks and sidelines should be loose but not sloppy at first and the pony allowed to wear the rig for twenty minutes a day in his box stall or paddock. Gradual tightening of the sidechecks raises the pony's head while the sidelines pull in and tuck his muzzle, giving an attractive head set and appearance to the pony. The bitting rig is worthwhile for all ponies but is particularly necessary for the harness show pony.

spring weather arrives unless you have indoor facilities. You begin by accustoming the pony to the bit. For this you will need a bitting rig which includes a back pad. If you don't have one, you can use a harness saddle satisfactorily.

Slip the bridle with the mouthing bit onto the pony several times until he becomes used to wearing it for half a day or so. During this time you can attach the back pad lightly to the pony's back, and at the same time get him used to wearing a crupper under his tail. Be careful the first time or two that the pony doesn't kick you when you attach the crupper and don't tighten it too snugly to the back pad in the beginning.

After he's become accustomed to the bit, back pad, and crupper, the fine harness pony should wear a couple of leather side checks running from the back pad to the bit rings like reins. These should have rubber bands or springs on them so the pony has some flexibility. Even though he fights them, they will always pull his head back into position and arch his neck in the desired manner. Also, this pulling action teaches the pony to drive much easier later. His mouth should be checked each time the bit is removed to make sure it is not soring his lips in any way.

If your prospect is to be a roadster or trotting pony, you must use an overhead check instead of side checks. Rather than tucking his muzzle, this will raise it into the racing position. This check runs from the top of the bridle to the back pad and should be tight enough so that the pony's head cannot be lowered below the back bone line of the body. With the racing pony the nose must be held out as far as possible as this helps in breathing, when the animal is working at top speed.

Basic training for the driving pony consists of long lining him from foot, that is, teaching him the rudiments by driving him with a pair of long reins that have you twelve to fifteen feet behind the pony and out of kicking distance. These reins may be web or nylon rope, and in the beginning it is best to put a halter over the pony's bitting rig and hook to each side of it rather than to the bit rings. If you have to pull sharply to restrain the pony, it will not affect his mouth.

Run the lines through the side terrets on the back pad or through the shaft bearers if you are using regular harness. The point is to keep the lines low in the beginning so if the pony tries to turn and face you, the

Long-lining the driving pony. This basic training precedes hitching him to shafts.

When you lead a harness pony to the shafts, stack the lines back and forth over his back. To harness your pony, put the bridle on first, then the breast collar or hame, back pad and crupper.

lines wrap around his rump and you can pull him back straight again. If the lines are high, he will turn right under them.

Harness ponies are long lined in square or rectangular pens forty to sixty feet on a dimension. Fluffed straw about two feet deep is placed around the edges and the pony driven in this to develop high leg action. Roadster ponies and particularly racing ponies do not require as much action as fine harness ponies, so they may be long lined in a paddock, ring, or pasture, although you'll want some sort of fence or wall to aim them at in order to develop their turns.

Have an assistant to help you in the beginning. That person will walk

beside the pony with a lead. When you start forward, give the pony whatever command you intend to use for this, like "Get up!" Your assistant
steps out briskly and the pony will follow, either instinctively or with a
little tug on the lead. Carefully practice turning the pony to the left
and right, advising your assistant each time so he can guide the pony
in these maneuvers. Work your pony ten minutes, let up on his checks
and praise him if he has done well, then proceed for another ten minutes.
Be sure to end up with the pony doing his part correctly.

You should carry a whip in your right hand, and if you have to use
it to make the pony go forward, make it a sharp blow, not a lot of constant tapping. When you start the second half of your training session,
begin teaching the pony to back. Let the assistant stand in front of him
and urge him to move back a couple of steps by applying pressure on
the reins and tapping the pony's front legs or knees if necessary.

Gradually work this training session up to half and three-quarters of
an hour. At this stage the pony will not be hot enough to require cooling
off afterward.

Remember to let him run an hour or so beforehand in the paddock
to get the youthful spirit cooled off, or else lunge him.

When the time comes to hitch him up, if you find he is still a bit wild,
attach a couple of long poles like shafts to each side of his back pad.
Drive him around with them dragging until he gets used to them. The
fine harness pony will need to be hitched to a buggy, the roadster and
racer to a jog or training cart. Here again, you will need an assistant to
help you in the beginning. Hitch up the first time in a large ring or
pasture. Your pony will learn to turn easier if he doesn't have to turn
sharply.

Drive the pony over to the vehicle so he can see it, then stop the pony
and hold him under a good firm hand while your assistant brings the
vehicle around and works the shafts into the shaft bearers. Don't tie them
down at first. He can hold them in place while you move the pony ahead
slowly and let him get the feel of having something behind him. If he
lunges forward, the assistant can let go of the shafts and the pony will
become disengaged with no harm done. A little time, patience, and force-
fulness should have you driving the pony while you walk behind the cart.
Guide him into large circles and figure-eights. Again, fifteen or twenty
minutes of this is enough, but end on a happy note, not a sour one.

After a few days you can carefully mount the vehicle and begin serious
training. From the beginning of his training, the fine harness pony should
be taught to stand spread and mannerly when he stops, as should the
roadster. This is not necessary with the racing pony. The fine harness
and roadster ponies will wear blinders on their bridles, the racing pony

The roadster pony has three gaits, jog, road gait, and turn-on, all different speeds of the trot. Here, X-Tempo, a Shetland roadster stake winner and high-point roadster pony in the Pacific Northwest in '62, '63, and '64, displays fine style in the road gait under the guidance of professional trainer Joe Biles. Note the driver's hands and position of the whip.

Opposite:
Position of hands when driving is important. Top illustration shows the most popular way of holding lines. Lines (a and d) run from bottom of fists through palm and out between index and middle fingers with the bite (b and c) falling loosely in lap of driver. Whip is cocked smartly just off the vertical. For turning either right or left, that particular hand is drawn slightly closer to the body and the other one eased forward a bit. To stop, the hands are curled firmly toward the body as shown in the center illustration. The lines (a and d) are tightened while the bite (b and c) falls loosely in the lap. Bottom illustration shows the most popular way of driving a four-in-hand. Lines 1 and 3 are for right turning, 2 and 4 for left. The right hand is free for the whip and other maneuvering. When a turn is desired, the right hand takes hold of the proper pair of lines and draws in on them, turning the ponies in that direction.

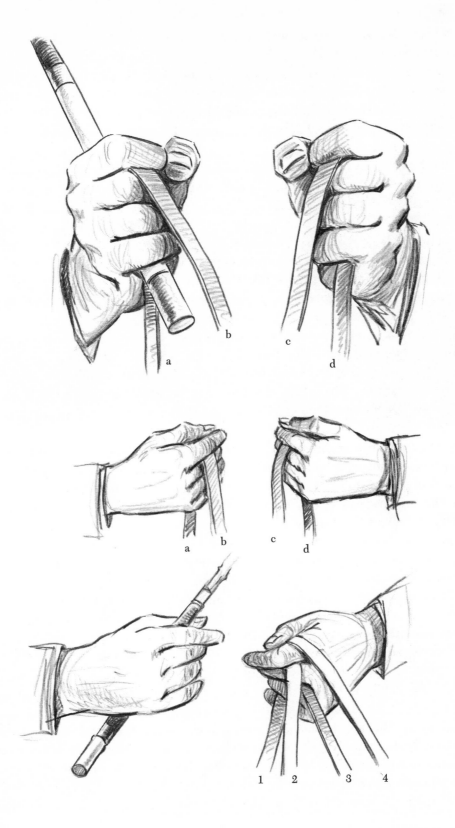

a   b   c   d

a   b   c   d

1   2   3   4

will not. No pony should wear his best harness in training. It may get broken or stretched.

The harness show pony must be able to back, but don't try to make him back from a standing stretched position. Teach him to take a step forward, then to back promptly and straight, without any fussing.

There is a proper and safe way to mount a buggy. It is done from the near side with the reins held tightly in the left hand, the whip in the right. The driver always sits to the right side of a vehicle and holds the reins in his left hand. The whip should be carried at an angle above the pony and above the face of any passenger. The driver should sit well back in the seat with feet forward and well braced. He should look straight ahead, watching his pony's every move. Control is concentrated in his left hand; turns are made by the fingers of the right hand. Variations in gait are compensated for by a little give or take in the reins. The only contact you have with the pony is through the reins which must carry all the necessary signals and directions. This is the art of driving.

Most fine harness ponies wear a Liverpool bit which has a bar with three slots called the half-cheek, first curb, and second curb. The reins can be buckled into any of these or inside the circle, which then makes the bit a snaffle. The lower the lines are buckled (second curb is the lowest), the stronger the bit becomes and the judge realizes that the pony is hard-mouthed.

Harness ponies are permitted to wear humane or false tails. The frame for this is attached to the crupper just above regular tail and the artificial one hung over it so neatly that it is nearly impossible to identify.

The fine harness pony is more or less a product of the professional trainer whereas the roadster is nearer to a do-it-yourself pony. The equipment is less expensive, the shoeing less complicated, the racing silks colorful, the showing procedure great fun because you don't have to ride around in controlled dignity during the class but can really let yourself go.

The roadster doesn't require the exaggerated action of the fine harness pony. Of his three gaits, the jog, trot, and turn-on or racing gait, the first two are his most animated, the third is for speed. The procedure is for the roadster to enter the show ring going to the left at a jog, then progress to a road gait. He is then reversed at a jog, goes into the road gait, and finally is turned on for speed. Thus his training should follow this pattern. You'll have to work him miles and miles to perfect his gaits.

Develop the jog first, then work on the road gait, an intermediate speed. Then go back and forth from one to another. Once he is in condition and warmed up, begin to turn him on and build up speed. Keep him in form and make sure he doesn't break. Most show rings are oval and roadsters who go well on the straightaways tend to break on the

forging   *overreach*   *scalping*

The most common forms of interference are: 1. forging; 2. overreaching; 3. scalping. In many cases proper shoeing will correct these faults.

curves, so practice these extra well. When you take them at high speed, make sure to sit on the inside of your seat. This will keep you from flying off into space on turns and also help your pony maneuver them better.

When the line-up call is given, you will be sailing around the ring at top speed and your pony will still be excited as he stops. Since you are allowed no header (attendant), he must settle down mannerly and stretch. The judge is inevitably impressed by the whirlwind pony which comes roaring in and lines up like a gentleman.

Roadsters are driven to two-wheeled vehicles like sulky or bike. Their harness includes a low crupper, overcheck, square blinkers, and straight or broken snaffle bit. Boots and martingales are permitted. Remember that your harness is under racing conditions, so have a couple of straps and an extra pair of boots at ringside in case something goes wrong. You have seven minutes for repairs, but if you have to return to your stall you'll be out of luck.

It's only a stone's throw—or maybe a couple of toe weights—from a roadster to a racer. Many a good pony has made the switch in the last few years, and many more are likely to. The harness is practically the same except that the trotter doesn't wear blinders.

Conditioning the trotting pony requires skill and know-how. His feet are trimmed so they are a little long in front and stubby behind. This helps to avoid scalping (dragging the front toe over the rear hoof) and forging (striking the front heel or quarter with the rear toe). The pony is driven by a half-check snaffle (either broken or solid) and also wears a stiff wire check bit attached to the overdraw check rein. This latter holds the pony's nose out and head up as previously described.

When training on a track, the procedure is to jog in a clockwise direction along the outside of the track. Once you have warmed up and want to go at racing speed, you turn in against the rail and go in a counterclockwise direction. But there's a lot of jogging and walking and jogging to be done before you can start pushing a green pony. The usual procedure is to start off walking for half a mile, then jog a half, then walk a half, then jog a mile, walk a half and jog another mile. In a couple of weeks you build up to jogging five miles or better per day. One nice thing about ponies is that you can cool them out by walking a mile at the end.

In a month's time your pony will be getting hard enough to carry a watch along with you. He should go a couple of halfs in 2:30 or 2:40. After this, you can start pushing him into the bit at the eighth pole. If he breaks, pull him up sharply. You have to push him not only to find out how fast he can go but also to develop him. Each time he breaks, pull him back sharply, then ask him to go on again. He'll soon catch on that he is supposed to trot and that breaking will be very uncomfortable.

It's wise, when you're jogging on the outside, to work with another driver and pony. You can teach your pony to trot close to a wheel and disregard the flying dirt. You can pull him out, bring him up alongside, then move him ahead, edge him over close to the other cart and drop in on the rail ahead. Then the other pony can pull out and pass. Criss-crossing like this teaches the pony that he must maintain his gait and speed even when another pony pulls in front and the wheels go right under his nose.

When the two ponies turn to the rail for a little speed, they can still practice pulling out and going around, only this time with more pressure on them. Coming home, they can really drive for the wire.

After the finish, don't turn your pony back until you've gone a considerable distance beyond the wire, for there may be other ponies barreling along right behind you. And never stop on the track unless you're full to the outside rail. Most accidents are caused by stopping or slowing down too quickly.

It's important to warm your pony up well before race time, but you don't want to take anything out of him. Try to warm up ten to fifteen seconds behind your pony's racing speed. You should have at least three half-mile warm-ups before race time, the last one coming about fifteen minutes before post time. Don't worry if he sweats a little, and have a blanket ready to toss over him to keep his body warm. Usually track rules require you to wear full silks if you're in the upcoming race but only a hat if you're warming up for future heats. You can always check this with the track stewart.

About shoeing your pony, the accepted theory among trotting horses is that the weight should be in front and the traction behind. Front toe weights are helpful to extend the stride. Consult a good blacksmith. He

In hitching a pair of ponies, someone should always stand in front of the two ponies to keep them steady. Note that driver on the left has a stout hold on the reins. He will enter the viceroy from the left.

can cut down and probably eliminate interference in your pony. Shoes should be reset every four or five weeks when you're racing.

Pony trotters generally need a minimum amount of booting. Ankle and quarter boots are helpful if needed, and sometimes a shin boot behind. Much more than that the blacksmith can probably remedy by changing shoes a bit.

A few driving tips:

Don't weave in and out. Not only is it illegal and dangerous but you're going much farther than necessary.

Be careful how you pull your pony up when he breaks. If possible, take him to the outside until he settles down. If you're in close quarters, remember those behind you. The rules say that you must lose ground on a break or be penalized.

At the start, try to get away and if you can't make the top, tuck in close as possible to the rail. This is the shortest distance to the wire. It's a proven truth of racing that the horse or pony out front gets the greatest amount of strain. If you can drop in behind a fast pony and a good driver he'll often bring you around at a speedier gait than you could have done by yourself. Then when you head for the wire, if everything else is equal, you should have more pony left than he has.

Good trotting!

Glossary

Glossary

Action – manner in which a pony moves his legs and feet.

Albino – pure white pony without pigmentation in hair, skin, or eye.

Amateur class – a class for those who ride or drive for pleasure as opposed to the professional who makes his living from the sport of ponies.

Appaloosa – a breed characterized by spotted or snowflake markings.

Auction – a public sale at which ponies are sold to the highest bidder.

Barrel – the body of the pony between the fore legs and hind legs.

Bay – a brown-colored pony with black mane, tail, and legs.

Bell boots – rubber boots put on the front feet of ponies for protection against overreach.

Blaze – a large white marking on a pony's face reaching from forehead to nose.

Blinkers – covers attached to a driving bridle to block the pony's side and backward vision so he will not be frightened of passing vehicles or disturbances.

Bottom line – the line formed by a pony's belly and lower neck, c.f. *top line*.

Broodmare – a female pony used exclusively for breeding.

Brushing – a slight interference caused when front hoof in being brought forward, brushes the hair to the opposite front leg.

Buck – the springing jump of a pony attempting to unseat its rider.

Buckboard – a four-wheeled driving vehicle for ponies or horses.

Buck-kneed – the front knee bends forward when the pony stands.

Cannon – the bone or portion of the leg between the knee or hock joint and the fetlock.

Canter – a slow, rhythmical, four-beat gait that, when extended, becomes a gallop, swiftest of all pony speeds.

Chestnuts – horny, harmless growths found on the inside legs of all ponies.

Cinch – a band around the belly to hold the saddle in place. Always check it before mounting.

Claiming race – a trotting race in which any of the pony entries can be bought for the allotted amount any time up till the race begins.

Clean – a pony is said to be "clean" when his legs are sound and free of blemishes.

Colic – an acute abdominal pain caused by gas in the stomach and intestines of a pony as a result of improper eating.

Collected – a pony is said to be "collected" when he performs a gait with good, balanced action.

Colt – a young male pony which has not reached full maturity (four to five years).

Conformation – the physical outline of a pony.

Cooler – a light cotton sheet put over a pony after a workout while he is being walked around to cool out.

Crest – the upper line of the neck.

Cribbing – the vice of chewing wood or gripping the teeth on something, extending the neck and sucking in wind.

Crossbred – a pony whose parents were purebred but of different breeds, i.e., Welsh and Hackney.

Croup – the upper rump of a pony.

Crupper – a harness strap running from the back pad down the back and under the tail.

Curb bit – a bit with straight or ported (curved upward in center) mouthpiece.

Curry – a blunt-toothed, oval comb of rubber or metal used for cleaning the very dirty spots on a pony's neck or body.

Dam – the mother of a pony.

Dappled – marked with spots lighter than the basic color of a pony, especially across the rump.

Docked tail – a tail that has been surgically shortened to make it appear more stylish as in the short-tailed Hackney.

Dressage – guidance of a pony through a set of maneuvers without perceptible use of hands, reins, legs, etc., although all these are used to provide signals.

Dwarf horse – a diminutive horse whose parents were full size, but through malfunctional development has little or no growth. Though small in height, he is not a pony.

Equitation – the art of riding, or horsemanship.

Extended – a pony is "extended" when at full speed or near so, in whatever gait he happens to be moving. His stride is long, leg action low and forward reaching, just the opposite of collected.

Fancy turnout – a driving class for children twelve or under who must wear specified afternoon or evening attire.

Farrier – one who shoes ponies.

Feathers – a long hair growing on the fetlocks, typical of the Welsh.

Filly – a female pony, unbred and under four years old.

Fine harness – the flashy, lightweight harness used for driving ponies hitched to park vehicles like the viceroy.

Flank – the area of a pony between the last rib and the point of hip.

Flank cinch – the second cinch on a Western saddle passing under the belly at the flanks.

Floating – filing the teeth in an older pony to restore the bite.

Foal – a very young pony, unweaned and of either sex.

Forelock or foretop – the tuft of hair between a pony's ears which grows forward and down over his face.

Forging – striking the front foot or shoe with the rear foot.

Founder – a serious disease of the blood vessels in a pony's feet, causing severe lameness, often permanent.

Fox-trot – a broken or divided gait wherein the pony walks with his front feet and trots with his hind feet, a surprisingly comfortable movement similar to the running walk.

Frog – the soft "V"-shaped pad on the sole of a pony's foot.

Futurity – a racing or show event in which ponies are entered generally before they are born.

Gaits – the various movements of a pony's legs. They consist of primarily the walk, trot, and canter, secondarily the running walk, fox-trot, pace, and rack.

Gallop – an extended canter, the pony's swiftest gait.

Gelding – a castrated male pony, always more docile as a result.

Gestation – the period of time required for pony foetus to reach maturity, generally eleven months.

Get of sire – the offspring of a specific male pony.

Goose rump – a short croup sloping steeply down to the tail; undesirable in ponies.

Grade pony – a pony of unregistered ancestry, hence usually of mixed or undeterminable breeding.

Green broke – a pony that has been ridden or driven only a few times.

Groom – to clean your pony, either for showing or for pleasure riding.

Gymkhana – a organized contest for ponies and riders, including such events as musical chairs, keyhole race, stake race, etc.

Hackamore – a Western type bridle with no bit.

Halter – a leather or rope headpiece used for handling or leading a pony about.

Halter class – a show class in which the pony wears only a halter and is judged on his conformation and way of going.

Hand – a unit of measure for determining the height of a pony; each hand is four inches.

Hard-mouthed – said of a pony who has lost sensitivity to the bit in his mouth, hence is difficult to manage.

Heavy harness – the heavy-duty leather straps and collar used on a pony for pulling contests or weighted wagons. The opposite of light or fine harness.

Height – the height of a pony is the distance from ground to top of withers and is measured in either hands or inches.

Hinny – a hybrid resulting from a cross between a horse or pony male and a female ass. The reverse cross of a mule, they have none of the strength and utility of that animal.

Hobble – a short rope, leather, or chain attached to the front pasterns of a pony to limit his movement; used on overnight camping trips, allowing the pony to graze but not run off.

Hock – the rear knee of a pony, known as the hind leg tarsal joint; all forward movement and jumping thrust come from the hocks.

Hogged mane – a mane that is clipped short and close to the skin.

Hoof – the hard, horny covering of the foot.

Hopples – a leg device for pacing ponies to keep them from breaking stride while in a race.

Humane tail – an artificial tail consisting of a switch and wig, and forming the illusion of a set tail; used on driving ponies.

Hunting pony – one experienced in and used for foxhunting.

Inbreeding – the mating of close relatives of the same family to establish or maintain the superior characteristics of an outstanding ancestor.

Indian broke – a pony that will handle by a mouth thong instead of a bridle and allow mounting from either side.

In-hand class – same as halter class; see above.

Interfering – hitting the cannon or fetlock of one leg with the hoof of the other, a sign of poor conformation.

Jack – a male donkey or ass.

Jack spavin – a bony enlargement on the inside rear leg of a pony, as a result of a severe sprain.

Jennet or Jenny – a female donkey or ass.

Jog – the slow, easy trotting gait of a Western using pony or a racing pony.

Jog cart – a light, two-wheeled vehicle for training ponies to drive.

Jumping pony – a pony specifically trained for jumping at pony and horse shows.

Keepers – the leather loops on harness and tack through which the strap ends, after being buckled, are run to keep them neat and in place.

Knee-sprung – see *buck-kneed*.

Laminitis – see *founder*.

Lead – the rope or strap snapped to the pony's halter for leading.

Leads – at a canter, a pony will lead with his left or right front and hind feet. If he turns to the left, he should be on a left lead; that is, his left front foot should strike the ground before his right front foot, otherwise he will not be able to maintain his balance.

Lead team – the forward team in a four-, six-, or eight-pony hitch.

Leopard-colored – a white pony with black spots (not patches) over most all of his body, a very dramatic coloration.

Line breeding – a mild form of *inbreeding* (see) whereby not too close relatives are mated to maintain family characteristics.

Lines – the long reins used for driving a pony.

Liverpool bit – a popular driving bit for show ponies.

Lope – the low easy gallop of a Western using pony.

Lunge – exercising a pony on a long rope in a circle.

Maiden class – a class for ponies or riders who have never won a blue ribbon in this particular event before.

Mane – the long hair on top of the pony's neck.

Manners – the general behavior of a pony.

Mare – a female pony over four years of age.

Midget pony – one whose height at withers is 32 inches or less.

Model pony – one who is judged only on his conformation, generally said of Shetlands.

Mule – a cross between a donkey and a horse; a very durable and useful animal for farmers.

Muzzle – the nose of the pony.

Near side – the left side of a pony.

Neck reining – turning a Western using pony to the left by light pressure of the right rein against the right side of his neck, and vice versa.

Novice class – a class of ponies or riders who have not won three blue ribbons in this particular event.

Off side – the right side of a pony.

Overcheck – the long strap on a harness pony which runs from the back pad up the crest of the neck to the poll, attaching either to the crown of the bridle or continuing down the face of the pony and forking to the mouth to hold an overcheck bit. Its purpose is to hold the pony's head high, making him more attractive and allowing the driver more control.

Overcheck bit – the light, slender bit used with the overcheck.

Overreach – the distance the rear foot moves beyond the track of the front foot on the same side; said especially of Tennessee Walking ponies.

Pace – a two-beat gait in which the left front and rear feet move in unison, as do the right front and rear. Its speed is equivalent to the trot.

Paddling – in high-action ponies, the outward swinging of the hoofs and forelegs as though paddling the air; it is a fault usually the result of being pigeon-toed.

Pair of ponies – said of two driving ponies hitched side by side.

Palomino – a golden-colored pony with light or white mane and tail.

Parrot mouth – said of a pony whose upper jaw protrudes beyond the lower jaw.

Pastern – the small part of a pony's leg between the fetlock and hoof.

Pedigree – a paper showing the sire and dam, grandsires and granddams, and other ancestors of a specific pony; it may be written up by the owner or officially issued by a breed registry.

Piebald – a pony of black and white coloring in large patches.

Pinto – a pony with bicolored body markings in large patches.

Pole – the shaft of wood which rides between a pair of ponies and which steers the vehicle being drawn.

Poll – the top of a pony's head.

Pommel – the high front part of a saddle, also mistakenly confused with the horn on a Western saddle.

Prepotent – said of a pony stallion who has the ability to transmit outstanding quality and ability to his offspring.

Produce of dam – the offspring of a specific female pony.

Puller – a hard-mouthed, willful pony that is difficult to manage.

Purebred – said of a pony whose ancestors have all been registered and recognized as a breed for many generations.

Purse – the prize money offered to trotting ponies for a race.

Quality – the refinement and "good looks" in a pony.

Quarter boots – light, protective boots placed on the front feet of trotting ponies for protection against interference while racing.

Rack – a swift, man-made, four-beat gait performed by five-gaited Saddle ponies.

Rear – said of a pony who suddenly rises up on his hind legs with head and forefeet high in the air.

Registered – said of a pony who has been officially recorded in a breed registry and issued a certificate or "papers" to prove it.

Reins – the leather straps attached to the bit on each side of the mouth and used by the rider to maneuver the pony.

Reserve grand champion – the runner-up to the grand champion at a pony show.

Roached mane – trimming a pony's mane to form an arc of upright bristles extending from poll to withers.

Roadster – a pony trained and fitted just like a trotting pony, with sulky and racing silks, but he competes in show ring classes, not on the race track.

Roan – a color in which white is mixed with bay, sorrel, black hairs, or the like, giving a brindled effect such as red roan, strawberry roan, blue roan, etc.

Roman nose – a pony with a convex profile to his face, generally a sign of willfulness and coarseness.

Rump – the heavy rear muscles of the haunches and hips.

Running walk – the smooth, gliding, four-beat movement which is the famous gait of the Tennessee Walking pony.

Saddle sores – raw and/or infected areas on a pony's back caused by improperly fitted saddle or blanket.

Scrub pony – a pony of very low grade.

Seat – one's posture while riding.

Shafts – the poles on each side of a single harness pony which turn the front wheels of the vehicle being drawn.

Sickle-hocked – a defect in which the hocks of the hind legs are too flexible and thus extend too far rearwards.

Side checks – on a harness pony, leather straps which run like reins from the bit to the back pad and draw in the pony's chin, causing him to arch his neck gracefully.

Singletree – the pivoted or swinging bar to which the traces of a harnessed pony are attached; it is located directly behind the pony.

Sire – the father of a pony.

Skewbald – a name for pinto ponies which are white and any other color than black.

SMT – silver mane and tail.

Snaffle bit – the basic and most simple bit of all, always jointed in the middle.

Soft-mouthed – said of a pony with a very sensitive mouth which cannot tolerate jerking or sawing.

Sorrel – a yellowish-chestnut color.

Sound – a pony that is free of injury, defects, and blemishes is said to be "sound."

Spanish fiesta class – a costume class in which contestants dress in the manner of Old Mexico, and generally for Galiceños.

Spavin – a generic term for an enlargement or distension of the hock or adjoining area as the result of strain, concussion, or faulty conformation; the resulting lameness may or may not render the pony useless.

Stallion – a male pony generally used for breeding.

Stirrup – the circular toe-piece in which the foot is placed while riding; metal on an English saddle, wooden on a Western saddle.

Stock pony – another name for Western using pony.

Stretched – the show position of a pony in a model class, front legs slightly forward, hind legs to the rear.

Stud – a male pony used for breeding.

Sulky – a two wheeled cart used for racing of trotting ponies.

Surrey – a four-wheeled, two-seated vehicle for ponies or horses.

Sway-backed – a sinking or concave back, generally the sign of advanced age in a pony.

Swing team – the middle team in a six-pony hitch.

Tack – the general term used for riding and driving equipment, i.e., bridles, saddles, harness, etc.

Tandem – two ponies hitched one in front of the other instead of side by side as in a pair.

Temperament – the disposition of a pony with regard to the job he is trained for.

Terrets – rings on the top of the back pad of a harness pony; they act as guides for the lines.

Throatlatch – the strap of the bridle or halter which passes under the pony's throat.

Thrush – a disease of the frog of the hoof.

Top line – the outline of a pony from his ears down his neck and back to his tail.

Traces – the harness straps running from the collar to the singletree.

Trot – a medium speed, two-beat gait in which a front foot and opposite rear foot strike the ground together.

Tugs – the loops on the harness pads through which the shafts of the vehicle are passed.

Twitch – a rope loop on the end of a stick which, when slipped over an unruly pony's lip and tightened, will make him stand still for shoeing, clipping, or special medical treatment.

Type – the general structure and form of a pony which makes him typical of a breed or group.

Unsound – a serious fault, blemish, or physical disability which limits the use of a pony.

Viceroy – a single-seated, four-wheel vehicle with patent leather fenders and dash and chrome fittings, used for showing the highest quality driving ponies.

Walk – a flat-footed, four-beat gait, the slowest performed by ponies.

Wall eye – a glass, blue, or China eye; the iris is white from lack of pigment, and the pony may or may not have restricted vision.

Weanling – a foal which has been weaned from its dam but has not reached the January 1 following his birth, hence is less than a year old.

Weaving – a rhythmic shifting of weight from one side to the other, usually in the stall, a bad habit resulting from boredom and inactivity.

Western pleasure riding – riding a pony on a trail or in competition with Western saddle and bridle, using stock horse methods of handling, and dressed in Western riding clothes.

Wheel team – the team hitched directly in front of the wagon in a four-pony or larger hitch.

Wind-broken – a slightly roaring sound of wind being drawn into the lungs of a pony after galloping.

Wind-sucking – see *cribbing*.

Winging in – in high-action ponies, the inward swinging of the hoof, sometimes to the extent that it brushes or strikes the adjoining leg.

Winging out – the reverse of *winging in,* above; see *paddling.*

Withers – highest point of the shoulder, approximately where mane begins, and measuring point for determining height of pony.

WMT – White mane and tail.

Yearling – any pony past the first January 1 following his birth but not the second.

PHOTO CREDITS

Baytown Sun & American Shetland Journal, 10
Budd Studios, 16, 104
Collinson, 98, 101
Frank J. Cosner, 75 (above and below)
Ralph Crane, 57
Daily News, Welsh, West Virginia, 146
Wynne Davies, 79
Dee Photos, 42, 47
Freudy Photos, 19, 22, 56, 61 (above), 82, 180
Norman E. Grantham, 48
Jack Holvoet, 235
Polly Knoll, 139
Launspach, 61 (below)
Stephen Levy, 122
J. F. Malony, 25
Ernest L. Mauger, 68, 79, 83, 138, 140, 169, 238
M. E. Morris, 45
Jay A. McClasky, 41
Les Nelson, 126
Rabinsky, 248
Darwin J. Rhoten, 103
Shirley A. Rice, 86
Steinley Studios, 12–13, 18, 174, 175, 176, 177
Sargent, 64, 128
Willard Stewart, 71
Stoody Company, Whittier, California, 206, 207
Tarrance Photos, 73 (above and below), 74, 181,
    185
Western Farmer, 21
Thomas E. Wingfield, 110, 113
Roberts Zuege, 53

Index

Index